Praise for
The Slumber Party from Hell

by Sue Ellen Allen

"The memoir you hold in your hand is a labor of love, a healing process, a gift to the women that are still behind bars, and a gift to us, about a subject not spoken about enough in society: the central role that prisons, and the attendant political and economic structures that make their presence seem inevitable, natural in fact, play in society; the large amounts of money that are spent to incarcerate rather than educate, to punish rather than rehabilitate, to dehumanize rather than heal."

Alan Eladio Gómez, PhD.,
Borderlands Scholar and Assistant Professor,
School of Justice and Social Inquiry, Arizona State University

---

"In *The Slumber Party from Hell*, you live her experiences as Sue Ellen Allen takes you behind the prison wire. You are allowed to reflect on the lessons at the end of each chapter of this valuable book. Sue Ellen uses her tragedy to elevate human consciousness through gritty, visceral writing that involves our senses. She lives her motto. She has been there, done that, and now challenges us to help the next person suffering."

Raúl Sánchez Monreal, Jr., International Author,
One Hundred Drops of Water,
Principles of Life, Challenges and Inspirations

The Slumber Party from Hell

a memoir

by

Sue Ellen Allen

INKWELL PRODUCTIONS
Scottsdale, Arizona

Slumber Party from Hell

First printing: August 2010

ISBN: 978-09829589-2-6
Library of Congress Control Number: 2010935629

Published by Inkwell Productions
10869 N. Scottsdale Road # 103-128
Scottsdale, AZ 85254-5280

Tel. 480-315-3781

E-mail: info@inkwellproductions.com

Website: www.inkwellproductions.com

Cover: While in prison, the author lost all her hair to chemo and
the prison gave her an orange beanie as a covering. One side of
the cover reflects that time and the other, the woman she is today.

Printed in the United States of America

Dedication

To David, who started me on this journey.

To Gina, who lives on in my heart.

To Chris, Diane, Trevor, Mariah, Gianna, and Noah,
Gina's family, who made me a part of theirs.

To Eleanore and Will, who gave me my life back.

To Michele, who saw me as a human being and said yes.

To the original interns from Arizona State University, who helped
to build GINA's Team:
    Connie, Gladys, Leah, Liz, Maria, and Sarah.

To Gabie, Travis and Stephanie, whom we never forget.

"Bad things do happen; how I respond to them defines my character and the quality of my life. I can choose to sit in perpetual sadness, immobilized by the gravity of my loss, or I can choose to rise from the pain and treasure the most precious gift I have - life itself."

Walter Anderson

"The worst day of freedom is better than the best day in prison."

Anonymous Inmate

Table of Contents

Forward

I first met Sue Ellen Allen on Sunday, February 28, 2010, at the 9th Annual Local to Global Justice Teach-In, at Arizona State University. When the presentation, "Towards an End to Incarceration: A Prison Story," was over and opened to discussion, hands raised and one of the first persons to speak began her story with "I spent the last seven years in Perryville prison . . . " Sue Ellen was in prison in Arizona, but she could have been talking about any prison in America. The system replicates itself behind every wall. Her forthright honesty about time served was a prelude to a number of suggestions based on her own personal experience, and the experiences and memories of the women that are still behind the wall. After the session, I approached her and introduced myself; we decided to share a table for lunch; two GINA's Team interns joined us. We haven't stopped talking since.

The memoir you hold in your hand is a labor of love, a healing process, a gift to the women that are still behind bars, and a gift to us, about a subject not spoken enough about in society: the central role that prisons, and the attendant political and economic structures that make their presence seem inevitable, natural in fact, play in society; the large amounts of money that are spent to incarcerate rather than educate, to punish rather than rehabilitate, to dehumanize rather than heal. Because prisons are so invisible, their organizing power over society so hidden, it is that much more difficult to have an honest discussion about how much the system is costing our families, our communities, and our world at large. From my experiences teaching about incarceration and justice, many folks assume that 1) the criminal justice system is just; 2) that guilty is an existential category eliminating even the possibility of change; and 3) that the direct relationship between socio-economic experience and opportunities for dignified education or work can be ignored. Prisoner is "bad" by definition, and therefore not only unworthy of empathy, but unredeemable, static, immutable, dead, disposable; these are the views society generally has of people behind bars.

These are stories of hope and pain, frustration and anguish, anger, laughter and moments of happiness woven through and across the "time done" behind bars in Arizona. It is also an inter-generational story, lessons that also listen and provide glimmers of possibilities, a sense of humanity in the face of a machine that ends up crushing the human spirit, families, communities – all under the banner of "law and order" and public safety.

The overarching themes of the memoir emphasize the daily systemic emotional violence, as well as moments of collective and personal human dignity, experienced by women in prison every where. Sue Ellen's own experience was marked by her battle against breast cancer and the unimaginable process of beginning the intense and debilitating treatment in Maricopa County's Estrella Jail and continuing it in prison. But the death of her celly Gina Panetta at the age of 25 from undiagnosed Leukemia transformed Sue Ellen's life and how she "did" her time. She explains that at length. Gina's spirit blesses these stories but also haunts (this is not a bad thing) our present, reminding us that we can all be part of dismantling the prison regime.

"Been there. Done that. Now how can I help?" This is the motto for GINA's Team, for Sue Ellen. With ASU professors and a handful of interns, support from public officials, clergy, and volunteers, Sue Ellen has organized a structure that provides educational opportunities for women behind the wall. She found her passion in prison and inspires this in others with her straightforward honest renderings from her perspective about her own personal and shared "Slumber Party from Hell".

Listen to these stories. Listen to Sue Ellen. Listen to Gina. Then ask yourself two questions: Why am I not incarcerated? (And if you say, "I do not commit crimes," rethink that statement.) And what can I do to lessen the impact prisons have on society? At the end of the book, there are questions to ponder and discuss. Never has there been a better time to begin this dialogue.

Alan Eladio Gómez, PhD
Borderlands Scholar and Assistant Professor
Justice and Social Inquiry
Arizona State University

2

Acknowledgements

The main lesson I learned in prison was gratitude. There have been so many people on this journey who have held out a hand to me and helped me along the way. Every woman at Estrella and Perryville who helped me when I was down and showed me a loving heart. Every staff member who saw me as a human being. Every religious volunteer who came in the name of love. Every person who has said *Welcome Home*. I am deeply grateful.

Thank you to everyone who reached out to me from the real world when I was behind bars: Rochelle Balch, B.J. Boulter, Kris Bowen-Reed, Carolyn Cooper, Jane Page Crump, Donna Dwelle Marcum, Simon Gascoigne, Tracy Klucina, Carmen Lykos, MaryLee Merritt, Susan Ratliff, Hester Hill Schnipper, Chris Smith, Carol Wood, and Toni McElvain, Gina's Aunt Toni who typed all the original essays.

Thank you to those who see my vision and believe in me: William Anderson, Representative Cecil Ash, Patricia Brooks, Doris Coté, Isadora Dahlen, David Delozier, Sara Dobie, Billie Fidlin, Misty Hyman, Barbara H., Don (D.J.) Johnson, Mercedes Kee, Brandon Keim, Tom Lagana, Carol Manetta, Raul Monreal, Marianne Petrillo, Katie Puzauska, Ginny R., Naomi Rhode, Karla Roberts, Representative Kyrsten Sinema, and Maureen Williams.

To my sisters who keep me sane and laughing: Dalia Brandess, Renée Morgan Brooks, June Cline, Laurinda Cummin, Martha Navarro, and Peaches Sloan.

To Dr. Omer Reed who gave me back my smile.

To Annika Feder for her love, friendship, and creativity.

To my publisher, Nick Ligidakis, who believed in me.

Prison 101

Most prisons are designed rather like a wheel with a central complex and wheel spokes that comprise the individual yards where the inmates live. The central complex of Perryville Prison houses the administrative staff offices, the meeting rooms, the main Medical department, the central kitchen, inmate intake, and some isolation cells.

The individual yards house the inmates and include more staff offices, more Medical offices, education classrooms, a visitation area, a library, kitchens, and dining halls.

There are seven yards at Perryville:

- Lumley, a maximum security yard

- Santa Cruz, a medium security yard

- San Pedro, a minimum security yard

- Santa Maria, a minimum security yard

- Santa Rosa, a minimum security yard

- Piestewa, a minimum security yard

- San Carlos, a new minimum security yard, opened in 2010 to house 1000 women. It gives them the capacity to house 5,000 women. When I entered Perryville in 2002, it was less than 3,000.

All the women inmates in Arizona are housed at Perryville except for a small group housed at SACRC (Southern Arizona Correctional Release Center) in Tucson.

Introduction to the Journey

What if I'd never known you? When I think about all the people I've known, I'm amazed at our connectedness. One person leads to another and one connection leads to things we can't even imagine. Sometimes the very worst person or event leads to something magical.

If I hadn't moved to Phoenix, I wouldn't have met my husband, and I'm sure I wouldn't have gone to prison. But if I hadn't met David, I wouldn't have the best memories of my life — picnicking in Oak Creek Canyon, walking the dogs, working in the garden, dancing in the dining room, holding hands at the movies, making jam and a mess in the kitchen. I wouldn't have met the nicest, most caring, decent man I've ever known.

If I hadn't married David, if we hadn't had a business, if we hadn't gone to Portugal, and if I hadn't gone to prison, I would never have met Gina or her family. If Gina hadn't died, we wouldn't be so linked together in this mission of ours.

Think about your life. What difficult person has been a link for you to a pearl beyond price? What painful event has helped you see life in a different way? What illness and suffering has given you a new and profound purpose to help others? Look around at those difficult people and ask yourself, *What if I'd never known you?*

Spiritual literature abounds with insights that remind us there is no such thing as coincidence. Everything is important, nothing is meaningless, everyone matters. Every person, place, or thing, no matter how wretched or painful, plays a part in our lives.

Gina Panetta and I spent six emotional, enlightening, intense months together as roommates at Perryville Prison for women, part of the Arizona State Prison Complex. We talked about life and death, my death. After all, she was a healthy twenty-five-year old, and I was battling cancer. We cried together over the meanness of the place and we laughed a lot too, and dreamed about the future. Then Gina got sick and two brief months later she was gone. I will never forget my disbelief, my frustration, my anger, and my grief. Gina was so beautiful and full of life. I know her presence in my life was a gift from God.

What happened after Gina died? Well, life went on in the monotonous, bureaucratic prison way, except when it didn't. From the first day I was incarcerated and experienced the horror, the meanness, the waste of human beings, I knew I had been given an opportunity, but it had no form. After Gina died, as I witnessed and experienced the continued mistreatment of seriously ill inmates, I knew my mission was to raise awareness so this would not happen again. Suddenly, I had an ally, Gina's mother, Diane. She too was devastated and determined that this must not continue.

We started to correspond and then she amazed me by asking if she could visit. If you haven't been in Diane's shoes, you cannot imagine the significance of that request. She was asking to return to the scene of the crime, to sit where she and Gina and Gina's children had visited, where there were so many memories. I was moved beyond words.

When Diane and Chris, her husband, were finally approved and arrived on visiting day, we held on tight to each other, tears coursing down our cheeks, remembering. We had never met, but I had been with Gina the last six months of her life when she was changing and growing almost faster than a blink, and I knew we were connected. We had so much to talk about. We laughed, cried, and remembered. A spark was born that day. Diane and I developed a warm, loving friendship based on our mutual love for her daughter and our desire to turn our pain into something meaningful. Together, in baby steps, we began advocating for change, bringing awareness to the public eye.

What if I'd never known Gina? Each person we meet, each path we choose, makes a difference, all leading to unexpected yet significant experiences. We are all linked, and one serendipitous meeting can lead to magic or misery. It was no coincidence I went to prison when I did and was put next door to Gina. I'm convinced there is a Divine Plan because I could not make this up. You can call it God, the Universe, there are many names for the amazing power that presents us with this gift of life.

So, think again when you look at the people who make up your life. *What if I'd never known you?* I didn't love prison, but I do love that I knew Gina; that I knew Valerie and Tracey, Melissa and Melanie, Candace and Elizabeth and all the rest; that Gina's family is a part of my life; that prison brought me friends whose depth and generosity of spirit astonished me. I see them now as human beings who made mistakes — human beings who now seek atonement and a better future.

Most people never imagine they will go to prison. However, most people are in some kind of prison of their own making. Usually it is a prison of fear — fear of addiction, fear in a marriage, fear in a job, fear of loneliness, fear of change, fear of self. Everyone is doing their own kind of time. This is the story of my journey through prison and fear and the lessons I learned. I hope you will come to see them as valuable lessons wherever you might be . . . *inside or out*

Chapter 1

Gina

I was supposed to die, not Gina. She was only twenty-five. I was fifty-seven. She had her whole life in front of her. I thought mine was over. Why did she die? Why did I live to tell about it?

Early on the morning of December 12, 2002, I arrived at Perryville prison in a cold, white MCSO (Maricopa County Sheriff's Office) van with several other women. Besides my battle with breast cancer, I'd been up all night in the jail in a freezing cold concrete holding cell, and I was tired, anxious, and numb. I had no idea what was in store for me. It turned out to be an unforgettable journey, one that filled me with fear, sorrow, and joy. I met people I never would have in my previous life and experienced things I would not have believed possible. Some were horrific, demeaning, and inhumane; some were wonderful. Gina was part of the wonderful.

I had been on the yard only a few days when a tall, lovely young woman joined me after dinner and asked if I'd like to go to church with her. I jumped at her offer like a drowning woman grabs a life preserver. It was the beginning of a brief and beautiful friendship that defined my prison experience. Gina was twenty-five, less than half my age, but for some reason, she decided she wanted to spend time with me, despite the age difference.

We walked the track together, sharing our life stories. As we walked those monotonous circles, I learned that she was from a nice, normal, middle-class family, but had become quite rebellious starting at fourteen. She began sneaking out her bedroom window at night and one thing led to another. She got pregnant and her life was changed forever. Like so many women before her, she picked the wrong men, was introduced to drugs, and ended up in prison.

It was obvious that Gina was very smart. Despite her pregnancy, she managed to finish high school and work while raising two children. (Yes, she'd had another.) She was articulate and insatiably curious. At the time, I had a very difficult roommate. She was a tiny thing, actually in prison for robbing banks in a clown suit. She had what prison calls *anger issues.* Abruptly, she would refuse to do something, mouth off to an officer, cop a serious attitude, and be whisked away in handcuffs to the yard office (the central administrative office for the duty officers), surrounded by the parade of staff that always accompanied such rebellion. I'd breathe a sigh of relief, sure that she was on her way to CDU, the Central Detention Unit, when out of the blue, she'd reappear. No trip to CDU, no ticket (a disciplinary punishment) — just a warning. I called her the *Teflon Kid.*

One day, thank God, they'd had enough and she was gone for good. Gina quickly asked if she could move in with me as my care-giver. She knew I was starting chemotherapy soon and needed someone to help me through it. I warned her it might be messy. She laughed. She had four children, (yes, she'd had two more before coming here), and she could deal with anything. And so it began.

Sharing that small room with Gina was the best time of my prison experience. She loved to write and assigned me the task of editor. Thirsty for knowledge, she never minded my critiques. She said, "I can learn a lot from you, Sue Ellen," and constantly picked my brain. Her poetry, letters, and short stories reflected an undiscovered talent. She had a lovely ability to write with an authentic and passionate voice.

We wrote together and I welcomed her feedback. This was the beginning of my *inside out* essays. Gina loved my writings and declared emphatically that someday they would be a book. "They need to be typed. My Aunt Toni types over 100 words per minute. She'll type 'em for you." Privately I thought, *Sure she will. Your Aunt Toni doesn't know me from Adam's house cat. Why would she do that?* But she forgot to ask and it never happened. I kept scribbling and wishing for a typewriter.

In prison, Gina found her way back to God. She admitted that previously she thought being a Christian would be boring, but then discovered that once she found God, she was never bored. Her life was full beyond her expectations, even in prison. She enrolled in Rio Salado College. She had a good job. She worked out. She wrote. And we talked endlessly, often into the late hours when prisons are at last quiet, sometimes shattering the peace with uncontrollable laughter. Do you remember when you were young, hanging out with your best friend, when you would get the giggles over absolutely nothing and could not stop laughing? That was us. We would start laughing over something completely ridiculous, and I would have to put the pillow over my head to muffle the sound. Those were the times I treasure.

Gina's mother was close to my age and Gina admitted they'd had a difficult relationship.

"I've heard this all before. You say the same thing my mom says," she observed.

"Well, we are nearly the same age. What's the difference? Why are you listening to me and not her?"

She thought about it carefully. "Not sure. Maybe it's just time."

Because of my advice, Gina grew closer to her mother again. They were both really happy about that. Later, Diane, Gina's mom, with tears in her eyes, thanked me for giving her daughter back to her before she died. For that alone, I am thankful I was there for her.

Gina had dreams. For such a young woman, her life had been extremely full and colorful. She wanted to change those colors. She dreamed of becoming a guidance counselor so she could advise other young girls tempted to go down the same path. In a brutally honest voice, she wrote a moving letter to a fifteen year old friend, detailing her mistakes. It has since been copied and handed out to thousands of young people who continue to be moved by her message.

Four months after we met, on April 19, 2003, Gina collapsed and was taken to Medical. Not surprisingly, the Medical staff ignored this red flag. After all, she was a healthy young woman with no history of illness. She was slim, athletic, and active so they passed it off, saying, "Come back in two weeks and if you're still sick, we'll believe you."

Day after day, she weakened. She said her throat felt like she was swallowing ground glass. Medical said it was strep-throat. She said her gums were bleeding. Medical said it was gingivitis. She said her head felt like it might explode. Medical said it was migraines, her sinuses, or allergies. Her color went from tan to gray, and she lost fifteen pounds. She looked like a tall stick. They gave her antibiotics, but no blood test, even though she begged for one. Her parents called and begged, too. Medical said, "Your daughter is getting *appropriate* treatment." That is a favorite word within the system that covers up a multitude of sins.

The last weekend before they took her to the hospital was spent in agony. Too weak to climb up to her bunk, she lay on mine. I held her in my arms and repeated the 23rd Psalm over and over.

The Lord is my shepherd; I shall not want.
He maketh me to lie down in green pastures:
He leadeth me beside the still waters.
He restoreth my soul:
He leadeth me in the paths of righteousness for his name's
sake.
Yea, though I walk through the valley of the shadow of death,
I will fear no evil: for thou art with me; Thy rod and thy staff,
they comfort me. Thou preparest a table before me in the
presence of mine enemies:
Thou anointest my head with oil; my cup runneth over.
Surely goodness and mercy shall follow me all the days
of my life:
and I will dwell in the house of the Lord forever.

Gina cried and moaned in pain. "Make it stop, Sue Ellen. Why won't it stop? Please, please, please make it stop." Desperately, I tried to get help and was threatened with a ticket. "If you don't knock it off, Allen, you'll be on your way to CDU." Finally, the officers called an Incident Management System, better known as an IMS, to bring Medical to the yard. Nurse Bob came grumbling down to our room, and suddenly it was filled with staff all waiting for him to do something. It was June and already more than 105 degrees outside. There was no air conditioning and the room was unbearable. I begged him to take her temperature. Although they aren't supposed to touch inmates, one of the officers actually felt Gina's forehead and confirmed that she was *on fire.*

Stubbornly, Nurse Bob refused to produce a thermometer, despite the huge bag he carried, and left in a huff, angrily proclaiming there was nothing he could do. Just as quickly as staff had arrived, they vanished, and we were left alone in a small, hot concrete cell without comfort or compassion. Gina continued to get worse and, on the following Tuesday, they finally took her to the hospital. The doctor told her parents they had never seen a case like this. Gina's white blood count was 300,000 and her red blood count was zero. *(The average range for a white blood cell count is 4,300 to 10, 800 cells/per micro liter per cubic millimeter. The average range for red blood cell count is 4.2 to 6.9 million per micro liter per cubic millimeter. www.Bloodbook.com.)*

Her body was shutting down. Thus, her excruciating pain. Gina went into a coma and thirty-six hours later, on June 19th, two months after her first collapse, she died of undiagnosed acute Myloid Leukemia.

Nooooo! This was not supposed to happen. I was the one with cancer. During those long night time conversations when we'd talked about death, it was not hers, never hers. I alternated between shock and grief. I felt alone and helpless. We are "the property of the State." They are responsible for us. They are supposed to take care of us. How could they betray us this way?

I grieved. We all grieved. She was too young, her pain was unnecessary, and her death was tragic.

I wrote her parents to let them know what had happened. Our correspondence became a friendship. Eventually, they came to visit, although how they ever got the courage to come back to the prison, I'll never know.

One day, about six months after Gina died, I got an unexpected letter from a woman who introduced herself as Gina's Aunt Toni. "I know all about you from Gina's letters," she said. "Diane and Chris have told me what you did for her. I want to do something for you. I type 100 words per minute. Do you need anything typed?"

Angels are everywhere, aren't they? Toni's offer gave form to the stack of essays I'd already written and also helped me wrap my mind around Gina's death. It felt like Gina reaching out to me, "See, Sue Ellen, I didn't forget."

When I walked through the doors of the sheriff's horrific jail in July 2002, I knew I was there for a purpose. I knew this was part of my life's journey. It was much, much harder than I expected and many times I prayed for relief, but each day exposed me to new experiences that all led to Gina.

Gina's death was crushing. It made no sense, like so much of prison life, and I'm a person who wants to know why. There was, of course, that age-old question, where was God? Where was God in the hurricane that swept through New Orleans, the cyclone that leveled Burma, and the earthquakes that rocked Haiti and Chile? Where was God in Gina's death? Where was God in this slumber party from hell?

At the time of her death, I didn't know the answer. I didn't know that Gina's death would be the defining moment in this incredible journey. It caused me to think about it all and long to find meaning in the tragedy. Gradually, I did. Gina's death was a betrayal and this betrayal caused me to think of others.

Gina's letter to her 15 year old friend.

Dear Rory,

I am writing to you to share my life story in hopes that it will help you in some way. I come from a good, Christian family who are working middle-class. I was never abused or neglected, unlike so many of the other girls here in prison. My parents worked hard and were very loving. Perhaps their only mistake was not enforcing real discipline upon me.

When I was fourteen, I had an older boyfriend. I got pregnant that year. I should have talked to my parents (or any other adult close to me) about what was going on in my life. They could have helped me and maybe I wouldn't have gotten pregnant. Telling my parents that their baby was going to have a baby was frightening and shameful.

Once my son was born, I felt so out of place because I wasn't a regular teenager any longer, nor was I an adult. I was fifteen years old and I didn't fit anywhere. I ended up marrying my boyfriend the next year, partly because I felt it was the right thing to do and partly because it was a way out of my parent's house. The marriage didn't last long because he wasn't ready to grow up. I left him and found myself a single mom at seventeen. Unfortunately, I also found out I was pregnant again. Birth control, I discovered, isn't foolproof.

I was working and had an apartment. I managed to finish high school, but I couldn't make enough to pay bills. I was too stubborn to go back to my parents' house. I felt I had imposed on them enough. Besides, I was supposed to be a big girl, right? While my old friends went to parties and the prom and got ready for college, I had two babies to take care of. Those teenage years that I cheated myself out of can never be replaced. I'm just now realizing how important those years are to young people and what an impact missing that experi-ence has had on me.

Anyway, I was desperate to make it on my own. A "friend" suggested I could get a job as a dancer (stripper) to make enough money to live on. Finally I tried it and found it was degrading and yet exciting at the same time. The money was fast and easy. I got a big house, a new car, and did a lot of shopping! What I didn't real-

ize was the damage I was doing to my morals, my standards, my image, my self-esteem, not to mention the dangers of that environment. My intentions of going to college were forgotten. At this point, I was an eighteen year-old single mother of two children whose future was being sacrificed by my chosen "career."

It was during this same year that my now ex-husband got into a car accident because he was drinking and driving. It was devastating. He suffered massive head trauma. When I first saw him at the hospital, my knees buckled and I vomited. His head looked broken; it was so swelled up. He had staples all over, holding him together. His eye socket bone was broken, his jaw was busted in several places, and he was hooked up to so many machines. The doctors thought he would die within a few hours. Instead he survived, but for months he was in a coma. When he finally woke up, he didn't recognize any of us, couldn't feed himself, couldn't do anything; a full grown man in diapers.

Over the next year, he learned how to do all those things again, and one day I went to see him and he saw our baby daughter. There was recognition in his eyes. His memory came back more each day after that. Today he works full time, but he lives with his parents and probably always will. The girl who was in the car with him suffered a broken back and will never walk again. Such are the consequences of drinking and driving.

When I was nineteen, I met and married my second husband. Let me warn you that people are not always what they appear to be. Anyway, for a short while our marriage was great. I quit dancing, got pregnant two more times and enjoyed life. Somewhere along the way, he and I started doing drugs. I used to think pot was no big deal, but once you start smoking pot, you will surely find it acceptable to try other drugs. The best advice I can give anyone is NEVER try dope. You're not missing anything if you don't ever get high. Trust me on this one! It starts out fun, but it will end up as pure misery. I got addicted like most people do. Being addicted to a drug is the most agonizing thing I've ever experienced. Addiction happens fast and it's sneaky. You don't even realize you're addicted at first. I started doing more and more drugs. Eventually, I went back to dancing because supporting a habit is very expensive. Being an addict is like being in your own prison; the addiction keeps you prisoner. Drugs did not kill me, but they surely took my life. Addiction and criminal activity are a package deal.

To make the story of my crime a short one, let me just say I ended up on probation several times (it's easier than you think to mess up) and I was in and out of jail several times. Finally, I messed up for the last time and got sentenced to 3.5 years in prison. Custody of my first two children went to my first husband and his parents. My children from my second marriage are both now living with my parents. My second husband is still living the wrong kind of life and he can't take care of our children, but I continue to pray for him. My children are growing up without their mother, and I am missing out on more than you can imagine. The children all complain about missing me and not a single hour goes by that I don't ache to hold them.

Looking back, I realize that the choices I made at fourteen affected the outcome of my entire life and the lives of my family. I didn't realize it then, but the choices I made as young as fourteen were vital ones. I was selfish not to see ahead of time that getting pregnant so young would affect that child's life as well as mine. I was a good mother, but a lot of the time I felt as if I was just playing a role. Do you see what I mean? Until we're full blown adults, we're not equipped mentally or emotionally to handle having or raising a child. I think about all the babysitting and costs of the babies that were unfairly put on my parents, not to mention they are raising them altogether. Lesson: "The choices I make profoundly affect the lives of others."

I didn't have to teach myself how to become a drug addict, but teaching myself how not to be one is a long, hard process, one I may always battle. I am attending Rio Salado classes that are offered at the prison. That's the only good thing about this place. Most of the time I am locked in a small cell. There is no such thing as privacy. I wear the same uniform every day, eat the same nasty food, and the hours seem endless. My bed is a metal bunk with a worn out, skinny mattress. The guards are heartless, sometimes cruel, and so are most of the other female prisoners. I thank God for the few compassionate guards and for the few good friends I have.

I am isolated from the world and my family. I live life from behind a fence. The funny thing is, I feel free for the first time, free on the inside. Do you understand? I am one of the lucky ones who prison has affected in a positive way. I am stronger mentally, emotionally, and spiritually than I have ever been. This is rare though. Most of the girls here get caught up in prison life and never learn differently. And, by the way, strip searches are as degrading and humiliating as the first time you have one, no matter how many you have.

I want to become a high school guidance counselor. I will have to finish earning my degree once I'm released from prison. Once again, I'll be depending on my parents. My story and others like it don't just happen to the poor, the abused, or the bad. It can happen to anyone. It's all about choices. Please be careful to make the right ones, especially now at your young age.

I send this letter out with a prayer that it touches you.

Love,

Gina

Chapter 2

Betrayal

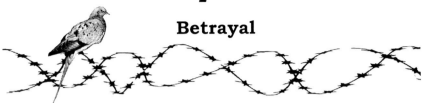

Betrayal in prison is common conversation, much like in the outside world. John Edwards, Elliot Spitzer, Tiger Woods . . . well, you know. The pundits love this stuff and each time someone falls, they have a celebration of chatter focused on the big question: Why do the wives of these men stand by them at the lectern and stick with their marriage? The entire gaggle of pundits (I just made that up. I have no idea what a bunch of pundits would be called, but gaggle sounds like gagging and that seems right) think these women should dump the bums immediately. No saint-like support, no counseling. Just kick'em out *now*.

To the pundits (and to many others), everything is black and white. In prison and in LIFE, I learned things are many shades of gray. Life is complicated. Nothing is ever as simple as the pundits make it. What about the years of marriage? What about the children? What about closure?

I know something about betrayal. I think my husband betrayed me, and my friends think I betrayed them. Sounds black and white, but it's not. The dictionary says betrayal is "to be disloyal or unfaithful." Such simple words for such desperate emotions. Nowhere does it mention anything about intention. What is the intention in all of this?

David lied to our shareholders when he inflated the projections of the company. He lied to me by not telling me what he was doing. Was his intention to steal for his own personal gain as the prosecution said?

No.

At trial, even the State said all the money raised went to the company. There was no personal gain. David was building a company that everyone believed in. We had a beautiful product of high end fashion jewelry, a fantastic sales team, excellent store placement, and big contracts. We were working like crazy to succeed for everyone. His intention wasn't to hurt anybody.

Now, from an investor's point of view, that doesn't matter. He lied, period. And I was devastated, furious, and deeply hurt. I couldn't eat, sleep, or function. So why didn't I leave? First, in my state of mind, I had no idea where to go. We had lost everything and I had no money. Second, it was my townhouse, so I could have kicked him out. He had nowhere to go either. So we stayed together.

Everyday when I couldn't get out of the fetal position, David was the one who lifted me out of bed and carried me to the shower. When I couldn't eat, David was the one who coaxed me to have just one bite. When I couldn't stop crying, David held me in his arms and cried with me, begging for forgiveness. There was no one else. The phone was strangely silent and I was afraid to call anyone; no money for the phone bill.

David was not my first husband and this time I had seriously vowed to make it work. No divorce. *But he lied!* He betrayed our investors who were family and friends. He lost their trust and mine. However, I knew his heart and I knew there was no plotting and scheming. There was no malice and never a desire for personal gain. He was building a company for everyone. I couldn't leave.

By not leaving, the world saw this as complicity. Surely there was pillow talk. *Surely, as close as they are, they must have planned this.* Only we didn't. No pillow talk, no plan. I believed in my husband, our product, and our company. Where David was concerned, my love was completely blind. I had put him on such a high pedestal, it's a wonder he didn't have a nose bleed. Of course, he fell off and both of us were broken in the fall. No one believed that I wasn't part of a plan, because I didn't kick him out. Not only that, I was painted as this brilliant Svengali, sweet-talking everyone out of their money.

Truthfully, if we had been so brilliant, we would have done better than the complete loss of our home, possessions, and reputation. If we had been so brilliant, long before any indictment came down, we would have left town with a million dollars in tow. But we weren't brilliant and we didn't leave for two years, because we were just struggling to survive. The money had been invested in the company; it wasn't lining our pockets. We weren't brilliant; we were well-intentioned. This was a hard-working man desperate to keep his company afloat and his wife a success. He didn't want to hurt me or disappoint me and, in lying, he did both.

If I was hurt, imagine how our investors felt. It wasn't just about money; it was about faith in a friend. It was about trust. They didn't invest in a company; they invested in me and they felt I betrayed them. I doubt if they will ever know how deeply sorry I am for their emotional havoc and their loss. The irony is that they believed in me enough to invest in me and yet later they believed I would betray them. I thought they knew me very well, knew my heart. It was devastating to realize that they felt I was capable of consciously plotting to take their money. David and I lived and breathed that company every minute of the day. Our only plotting was how to increase sales.

If the pundits can't understand how wives can forgive their husbands over infidelity, they certainly won't be able to understand how I could forgive David for creating this tsunami in our lives. After all, this is not about an affair; this is about going to prison, the worst experience of my life. However, it is also the defining moment of my life. Prison has helped define who I am today as a human being and has given my life a new meaning.

We never know what is at the end of a decision. No crystal balls. No Ouija boards. Something can seem disastrous and turn out to be a gift. Prison was a gift. It was not wrapped in a pretty blue box with a white satin Tiffany bow. I did not want to open it. It was an ugly, lonely, difficult, humiliating gift. I cried a lot. I hurt a lot. So why was it a gift if it was so awful? Good question. From the day I opened the box, I saw things I wouldn't have believed possible if I hadn't experienced them myself. I saw abuse, abandonment, cruelty, despair, fear, neglect, disrespect, and apathy. From officers and from inmates.

I also saw compassion, kindness, respect, generosity, and love in many forms. From inmates and from officers. In prison, not everyone is evil, violent, and brutal, nor are they all sweet, kind, and gentle. Prison is a microcosm of life, and the Bell Curve is alive and well in both inmates and staff.

My seven years there was a journey, the worst and most difficult in a life full of journeys. I would not wish it on anyone, but I would not trade it. It enriched me in indescribable ways. I learned patience and compassion. I learned what to treasure and what to discard. I learned that I belong to a dysfunctional family of people that I cannot turn my back on now that I am free. I learned who I am as a member of the human race. I learned that the only way forward is through forgiveness and love.

Surely those things are gifts and I'm not sure how you learn them without a whole heap of adversity. Some people listen to my story and lament, if only this or if only that, then you wouldn't have gone to prison. Waste of breath. It's my journey. It's the journey I was meant to take. It has given me my passion and my purpose in life . . . *inside and out.*

Chapter 3

Inside Out

July 2002. Inside Out, it's the way my life felt when I walked into my first jail. I was fifty-seven years old, a well-educated, well-traveled woman suddenly face to face with another world. I was afraid, shocked, and profoundly sad.

The first time they handcuff you is a shock. Some guards make them tight so they cut into your flesh at every move. Shackles are worse. They do what they are supposed to do; they restrict your steps and they are heavy and cruel on bare ankles. The holding cells are filthy, and there are only hard, concrete benches and an open toilet. At some odd hour, they bring salami sandwiches, but no trash bag so everyone just piles the trash on the floor. It helps feed the rats. They crowd about thirty-two women into an eight foot by twelve foot tank. It is desperately hot. Some are left to stand. No more room to sit or move. The theory is that this inhumane treatment will inspire people to not come back. It doesn't work. It just succeeds in dehumanizing them so they have no dignity or hope left.

I was kept there for twenty hours, waiting to be processed. The noise, the heat, the smell, the meanness of the guards, all contribute to a feeling of despair and fear. I didn't know such a place could exist in the United States of America — the beacon of civilization for the rest of the world. I didn't want to believe that human beings could create this hell and others were willing to work in it.

Finally, I was moved out to Estrella, the women's jail, with a group of other newbies. There our clothes were taken, we were strip searched, and given uniforms of black and white stripes. Then we were escorted to the dorms. I could feel the heat all the way down the hall. When we walked through the door at the end, it was like walking into Dante's Inferno. One hundred seventy-eight women in racks of bunks three tiers high. Eight showers that didn't drain and eight toilets. One sheet, one blanket, no pillow, one uniform, one bra, one pair of panties, one pair of socks. Anything else is contraband. Anything else is country club. Everyone sweats and smells and struggles to stay clean. The evaporative coolers broke down two months ago. Mid-July and 115 degrees outside, but no repairs in sight. Office air conditioning is fixed quickly, and the offices are kept freezing. The contrast is chilling.

The lights are kept low to ease the heat. Too dark to read and that is my only respite. Time feels upside down. The meals add to that. In the jail, there are two meals a day and the food is always the same. In the morning, breakfast is always a sack with bologna, six slices of bread, two slices of cheese, one old orange, and crackers. In the afternoon, dinner of unrecognizable mix and smell is served on a brown tray. The windows are small and very high so the only feeling of time is from the light. Meals are served at irregular times, and time is twisted. Tock Tick, Tock Tick.

It feels like a twenty first century concentration camp and, because of the heat, we are living in the ovens. Everyone in black and white stripes. Everything done to debilitate and demoralize. It is big business designed to create a revolving door of job security. Most inmates are poor. No one cares. The guards call everyone "Ladies," but their voices drip sarcasm and there is no place here for anything remotely lady-like.

I'm lucky. I'm older. I've had a lovely life. I've worked and traveled. I know what love is. I have wonderful memories. Too many of these women have only horrible memories. Too many have been abused by fathers, mothers, boyfriends, pseudo-uncles. They do drugs to escape the pain. Then, to pay for their drug habit, they sell their bodies and steal. They are so young, but most are already mothers, and their children are scattered to the winds of family, adoption, or CPS (Child Protective Services).

The first night in the dorm, one of my neighbors literally vomited her insides out all night long. I'd never heard such suffering and sadness. Heroin. Dear God, what an awful sound. I wondered how she could survive. This was my first exposure to drugs and it was horrifying. But drugs or no drugs, despite our age difference, the kindness of these drug-addicted women overwhelmed me. These young women shared their few possessions with a generosity unseen in the world that I had known. I was so profoundly sad and frightened, and they embraced and comforted me.

"Don't worry. You'll be safe. We respect our elders." They might be criminals to society, but their hearts were full of compassion. From these women, I learned that blessings can come from the least expected places and we should never judge . . . *inside or out.*

Chapter 4

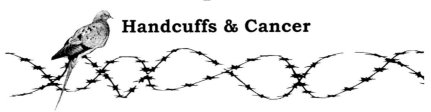

Handcuffs & Cancer

October 2002. Besides the normal fears of incarceration, I faced something different. On Valentine's Day, 2002, I was diagnosed with Stage 3B breast cancer. Religiously every year, I had a mammogram, but somehow in 2001, the lump was ignored. Then a year later, everyone suddenly jumps into full panic. Needle biopsy. Core biopsy. Tests, tests, tests. Lots of needles. Veins too small. Solemn faces. Who's the best oncologist? Everyone has a frightening story and a sure-fire unorthodox treatment.

So it begins. My oncologist informs me that the correct protocol for my case dictates eight sessions of chemotherapy every three weeks to shrink the six centimeter tumor. Then a mastectomy. Then five weeks of radiation. How do I feel? I feel okay. I can do this. Millions of women have survived this. Rally our friends. Pray. Start reading. Get educated.

I know that a positive mental attitude is crucial. Visualization. I visualize angels flying through my veins and body, killing cancer with laser lights. Friends send me pictures of angels, books about angels, and lots of prayers. I make jokes about the chemo *cocktail party* and some people think I am being too brave, but I don't know how else to be. Humor is healing, isn't it?

Chemotherapy is a six-day ordeal of blood tests, chemo, and nausea. Then normalcy and bliss for two weeks and then it starts all over. My hair starts falling out. Scary. Hair loss is a symbol of this disease, of death. It's painless, but it still hurts. I look in the mirror and don't recognize me.

At the end of June, with only two more sessions to go, our cozy world, our three dogs and four cats, vegetable garden, fresh food and pillow filled world collapses. Yes, we are living in Portugal illegally. Yes, we are blackmailed with violence and exposure unless we pay a very large sum of money that we do not have. I suppose we could have fled, but we agree it is time to go back. I take a deep breath and pick up the phone to call the American Embassy in Lisbon.

"Hello, my name is Sue Ellen Allen and I'm wanted in the state of Arizona for business fraud."

There is a very long silence. Finally, the person on the other end asks for my information.

"I'll have to get back to you."

Six phone calls and three days later the FBI calls from Madrid and we agree to meet them in Lisbon on Monday afternoon at two o'clock at the American Embassy. That gives us two days to prepare for the unknown. How naïve we are. We cannot begin to conceive what is in store for us. With cancer, life is frightening, but the penal system is a spiral into hell.

At the Embassy in Lisbon, we are treated humanely; in New Jersey, things are still civilized. In Arizona, however, the good manners stop. The sheriff there prides himself on running the toughest jail in America. It is designed to strip you of your dignity, self-esteem, and sanity. Into this I walk with balding head, collapsed veins, and trembling heart.

I walk into the heat and noise and confusion after thirty-two hours without sleep, looking dazed, feeling frightened, and much, much older than everyone. Barbara, a very pregnant young woman who looks about fifteen takes me in hand.

"Welcome to the slumber party from hell," she says.

She finds me a lower bunk and makes it the prison way. (A prison cot is thin, covered with plastic, and very slick. Sheets won't stay tucked under. They have to be tied a certain way or you'll be sleeping on a slab of plastic and a wad of cloth. Tying it right is a weird art, but you learn fast because your cot is your home.) I will never forget Barbara's kindness. It wasn't the last gesture of love and generosity that I would receive behind bars.

At first, enough tears pour down to float the place away. I cry from fear, I cry from pain, and I cry from great sorrow that such a place exists, created by man. In the movies, they always say crying in prison is a sign of weakness, something to avoid at all cost. On the contrary, I learn that tears always bring comfort, kindness, and love. The girls protect each other and they protect me. They bring me precious books. They share their meager possessions. There is indeed senseless cruelty and violence, horrible language, and stupid anger. But, for some reason, for me they shine. They clean up their language and live up to their potential. We have meaningful conversations and they are wonderful.

After living in this nightmare for two and a half months, the dreaded day arrives. Mastectomy. Not the way I pictured it. On September 26, at midnight, they wake me to shower and then I wait and wait. I feel so terribly alone, but I am ready. I know the drill. All the trips to the hospital are made this inhumane way. At two in the morning, I'm shackled, cuffed, and led to the bus with forty-nine other women for the fifteen-minute ride to the old jail and courthouse. We file into the old morgue that the girls call the dungeon. It is a big, cold, dirty concrete room with an open toilet on one wall. There are no chairs, just the freezing floor, so cold that it feels like an ice rink. There are little roaches everywhere, despite the cold, which you think would discourage them.

Fifty shackled women: some sit, some lie down on the filthy floor, some pace despite the shackles that cut into your ankles. We're all waiting for the door to open at four thirty. No books allowed. Time drags.

At four fifteen, we are moved upstairs, given plastic sacks of sandwich meat, bread, an orange, and blue Kool-aid. This is the only food inmates at court get for twelve hours or more. Daily bread takes on a whole new meaning. It is freezing in those cells. We shiver, we pray, we talk, we shiver some more while we wait for the dawn.

No food or drink for me before surgery. Instead, I wait. There are ten women crammed in each small cell with four bunks, no mattresses, just the cold, hard steel. For four hours, the women all sit, lie, pace, and pray. By eight fifteen, when the guard starts yelling names, we are all frozen stiff, sore, and exhausted. That is the condition of inmates as they go to court. They will be faced with some of the most important decisions of their life and they are exhausted before they start. So am I. Finally, I'm led to the hospital van, anxious and alone.

I think surgery is at ten o'clock in the morning, but they put me in another concrete holding cell alone and I wait and wait some more. At noon, I ask, "What's happening? How long?" They give me no answer. I am cold, hungry, scared. More time to pray and I hold a one sided conversation with God.

God, this would be a great time to take me home, to let me see the light, to let me rest in your arms. But, if I wake up, I'll know you aren't done with me yet.

About three in the afternoon, a guard comes to tell me they had an emergency, but I'll be going soon. I haven't eaten in twenty hours; I haven't slept. Freezing and facing surgery alone, I am afraid.

Finally, at four o'clock, I am taken down to Admitting and the Operating Room full of surgeons, nurses, and my guards. Still shackled, I put on the hospital gown. For the first time in three months, I see myself in a real mirror. My hair is just gray fuzz, I've lost twenty pounds, and my muscle tone is gone. I look like a stranger. I look at my breast for the last time. How do they dispose of it? Does it go in the trash? The girls say it's going to Booby Heaven.

Finally, it's time, time for the I.V. Dear God. Four veins collapse. Digging, poking, crying, shaking. Stop! It hurts. Please, please, knock me out first and do the I.V. in the O.R. Finally in the O.R., the shackles come off as I go under.

I wake up five hours later upstairs in the jail ward, bandaged and sore. But alive.

Oh, God, I get the message. You aren't done with me yet.

Five days of hospital vacation. A real bed, pillows, and hospital food. Three meals a day. Vegetables, salads, one jewel-like cherry tomato daily. I slowly savor it, delighting at its taste. Imagine how grim life is when you think hospital food is delicious. I have five days to lie in a blissfully quiet room and heal. I am so thankful.

Finally, time's up. The oncologist comes to tell me my margins aren't clean. They didn't get it all. He thinks possibly more surgery, then more chemo, then radiation. My heart sinks. That is so hard to hear alone. I miss my husband so.

Handcuffed again and shackled. Back to the van, back to the jail where the girls are waiting. They missed me! For five days, no one has touched me, except for the surgeons with their knives and the nurses with their needles. At the jail, the girls hug me and laugh and cry with me. They look at my scar and say stunningly bad words. They hold my hand and comfort me. How glad I am for human contact.

But the jail is hell. Everything is a battle. *Please, can I have a sheet, a towel, clean clothes?* Exhausted after surgery, I have to wait two hours for a sheet so I can lie down. It takes twenty-four hours and three guard shifts before I finally get clean clothes, despite my unbandaged incision and constant pleading.

I have a new claim to fame. Medical tells me I am the first woman in their department's memory to have a mastectomy while in jail. There is no policy, no compassion, no common sense. There is no place for me. Everything is a battle and I am exhausted.

After surgery, the surgeon says I need a pillow to cushion my arm and provide protection and comfort. No pillows allowed in jail. That would be luxurious, even for a cancer patient. I tell the girls and they are silent. I know they feel helpless; so do I. I can't even get Medical to check my incision, let alone find me a nonexistent pillow.

However, a couple of hours later, four young women come in to my cell with an order.

"Close your eyes," said Roxie, "and hold out your hands, Sue Ellen."

When I do, I feel something soft. I look to find the most beautiful pillow I have ever seen. It is light blue, tufted and fringed, made of the Kotex furnished by the jail. The women contributed their precious supplies and wove them together to form a tufted square. Then they used the small golf pencil that we are allowed for our writing tool to punch holes in the ends of the pads. They took thin strips from another pad to use as thread to sew it all around. Finally, they fringed the end material to give it that designer look. Honestly, I've had beautiful, expensive pillows in my life, but never one that held so much love, creativity, and generosity. I treasure that pillow and hide it under my smock when the guards come to search for contraband. At a terrible time in my life, it provides indescribable comfort and I will never forget it.

The surgeons decide against more surgery. Instead, I am supposed to re-start chemotherapy three weeks after surgery. My condition is serious. I lost my breast and twenty-eight lymph nodes and I am very vulnerable. I wait and wait, but Medical won't talk to me. It is nineteen days before anyone even looks at my incision. Then, because I am desperate and in tears, a new nurse takes pity on me and sees me on Sunday. She cleans away the tape and clips the stitches. No one tells me anything about healing or exercise, but I read up on it before I came to jail so I am self-informed. I know what to do, but still feel very isolated and alone.

Cat is my arm coach as I heal. Cat, the 5'2" hooker with a talent to set Hollywood on its ears. A beautiful diamond in the rough, Cat has a love-hate relationship with herself. "Stretch, Sue Ellen. Raise your arm higher, higher. You can do it. You can do it. Yea, yea, yea!"

Becka is my breathing coach. I breathe into this little plastic gizmo. Deep breaths, very deep. Becka has asthma so she understands. Dear, crazy, Becka, who comforts me when it hurts.

Monie is my bunkie. We pray together. She asks me questions that I can't answer. "You are always asking us what our dreams are. What's your dream, Sue Ellen?"

Silence. I am afraid to dream. Afraid if I have a dream, I will lose it again. Am I really afraid to hope? No, hope creeps softly from my heart. I can't control it. Thank God I have a hopeful heart.

This place is designed to kill hope, but somehow God fills my heart through the love and generosity of these women. This experience in this wretched, hopeless place is a weird gift that will go with me and perhaps inspire others in their battle with cancer. I will never forget it or these women, their faces, their stories, and their love . . . *inside or out.*

Chapter 5

Fear

November 2003. Someone told me there are 365 references in the Bible to fear. Basically, all of them say, *"Fear not, for I, the Lord thy God, am with you."* So, with my faith that I treasure, why am I always afraid?

It started in the jail where the incessant noise, violence, hostility, and indifference overwhelmed me. It is a hellish place for a healthy person. The black and white stripes and the conditions breed anxiety and stress. There are rules you don't even know about, and one hostile officer who is having a bad day can make yours miserable. I was brought up to respect authority and obey the rules, but these girls have no respect for anyone and will "go off" on anybody . . . inmate or guard.

There are lock-downs. There is pepper spray. There are brutal searches by the terrifying *men in black.* Why? Fights, drugs, who knows? I stay in my corner bed and read, read, read so that at least my mind can escape. The noise continues nightly until well past three in the morning and I long for silence. There is no silence. Instead, they yell at each other to be quiet.

"Shut up." "No, you shut up." "Shut the fuck up." "No, you shut the fuck up, bitch."
And so it goes, night after endless night.

Here's the irony. Every night at ten as the lights go out, a prayer starts. Lying on those hard, plastic mattresses, everyone says the Lord's Prayer together. Then this follows:
Now I lay me down to sleep, I pray the Lord my soul to keep.
If I should die before I wake, at least it will be on video tape.
Then the real noise starts and goes all night. *Amen.*

I develop an exercise pattern. First I shake and then I break out in a cold sweat, my heart racing. I later learn that these are panic attacks. I've never had one before. I've never seen people treated like this before. Many say they deserve it. Maybe so, but it seems to me if you take a dog and put it in a cage in the backyard, give it really vile food, yell at it all the time and kick it a lot, and then in a year or ten, let it into the house to socialize, you're going to have a very angry, confused, frightened, and hostile dog. That may not be a proper psychological analogy, but that was what I saw around me.

I learn to live in this hostile environment. I struggle to keep my sanity and my health. Right after my surgery, I make a trip to court for sentencing. I hate these trips. They are a marathon ordeal without sleep or food. Because I lost twenty-eight lymph nodes, I am at high risk of lymphoedema and have an official permit from the nurse in the Medical Department to Security. They are not to cuff my right arm. I show it to the guard who ignores it. He shoves it back to me and continues to cuff me.

"But, but," I stammer. "I've just lost my breast. I could get lymphoedema . . . " He refuses to listen.

"You could at least be gentle," I say with tears in my eyes.

"I am being gentle," he snarls. "You aren't lying on the ground bleeding."

I cannot understand such cruelty. I am devastated. But when I get back to the dorm much later that day, my old spirit kicks in and I do the unthinkable; I file a grievance against the officer. I know I am in the right. I had a proper permit and he was wrong.

The next day, I am suddenly surrounded by the terrifying men in black who demand I move while they search my *home*. There isn't much to search, but they turn the mattress upside down and shake out my books and letters. Finally I learn that they are look-ing for a red pen. They want to prove that I am the one who wrote that note and forged the nurse's signature. A red pen! Inmates are only allowed a two inch golf pencil. The very idea is crazy. Never-theless, they come back twice more, doing their best to intimidate me. It works. I am scared to death, but not scared enough to con-fess to a lie.

Later, I see the nurse in the hall. She tells me they questioned her several times as well, trying to get her to admit that the note was a forgery and she was trying to protect me. I realize then what an evil atmosphere I am in and count the days until I am out of there.

Finally, after six months in that hellish place, I am sentenced and the judge expedites my move to Perryville Prison because I still have not had any chemo. It was supposed to begin in mid-October, but the doctor tells me surreptitiously that the jail has delayed it, hoping to get rid of me and save the money. At Perryville, I tell this to the apathetic check-in nurse.

"Well," she says, frowning, "the judge can expedite all he wants, but you're in prison now and you can get in line."

At last, my chemo starts and I am very nauseated. The kitchen sends me trays of regular food and I am horribly sick. I struggle to walk the two blocks to the kitchen to beg for just broth or plain potatoes. Nope. Nothing they can do. On my way back to my yard, I collapse, vomiting.

An officer comes and asks, "Can you walk the three blocks to Medical. There are no wheelchairs."

"I'll try," I murmur.

One third of the way across the soccer field, I collapse and vomit some more. As I lie there, a sergeant comes toward me, asking disgustedly, "What's the issue, Allen?"

How do you answer that?

Cancer. Chemo. I'm sick.

I vomit some more. His shoes are eye level. Shiny. Not boots like everyone else. I notice he keeps them well away from me.

Weakly, I manage to pull myself up and continue across the field. No one helps me. By now, there are several more officers and a nurse. They walk behind me in a weird parade. I make it to the picnic tables in Visitation where I stop and vomit some more.

"Get somebody to clean this up," the sergeant barks. No vomiting on the rocks.

I make it to Medical where the nurse puts me in a room on a hard, cold leather table. She hands me a wastebasket and I continue to vomit. How can I vomit so much? This never happened when I had chemo outside. My oncologist was determined that my nausea would be minimal. In prison, there is complete indifference. The nurse comes with news. The doctor says he is too busy to administer the shot to stop the vomiting. Even the nurse is frustrated. She says there is no emergency. He is just doing paperwork. I vomit until there is nothing left and then I dry heave until I cannot lift my head. At last, an hour later, the doctor comes in, obviously irritated to have to deal with me. He acts like I am faking and reluctantly administers the shot. Eventually, I am sent back to my room alone.

I have three more treatments of chemo. Despite the rigid schedule, never is the medication ready on time, nor is the newly discovered chemo diet ready. I have to spend my sickest days walking the very long distance across the field to Medical, begging for what I am missing. When I am supposed to be healing, I am worn out battling for proper treatment. I cannot understand the indifference. These are supposed to be health care professionals, and I am so sick.

I lose all my hair again. I ask for a turban like my friend, Christine, has. (Christine has the same advanced cancer and had her mastectomy a week before I did. However, I was in the jail and she was already in prison. We both suffer from this staff disinterest.) Although Christine already has a turban, Medical looks at me blankly like they have no idea what I am talking about and sends me to Security. Not their responsibility. Security shakes their collective heads and says that it's a Medical issue. Back to Medical who refuses to see me. It's not them, it's Security. Sick and finally in tears, I face yet another sergeant. She must feel some pity for my futile efforts for she promises to talk to Ms. Bailey, the ADW (Associate Deputy Warden). I trudge back to my room exhausted.

A few hours later, there is a knock at my cell door. The sergeant appears with a blond lady in regular clothes whom I have never seen before. It is the ADW, Ms. Bailey. Very nicely, she presents me with a bright orange beanie that she's had the Garment Factory make for me. I am very grateful, but wonder why it is necessary to bat me around like a ping pong ball, wearing me out, diminishing me, emphasizing my helplessness here?

That's the real fear, my helplessness in the face of a Medical department that is incompetent and apathetic. As the property of the State, my life is literally in their hands and I've come to realize they don't give a damn. I am not a patient with cancer, I am an inmate with cancer, and that has hidden meaning.

Chemotherapy is finally over. Radiation starts. No more nausea. Burning instead. Meanwhile, Gina collapses. At Medical they treat her with the same hostile indifference that I experience. I know that sounds strange but it describes it perfectly. Gina had previously given me a little pep talk when I cried over my situation at Medical. "Come on, Sue Ellen. It can't be that bad."

Now she is abjectly sorry. "I was wrong. It's worse." She agrees that when you're sick, it's awful to be neglected and feel so helpless.

On June 19, 2003, Gina dies.

The last week of her life is spent in horrific pain, crying, terrified, neglected. Medical is hostile. No one listens. Gina lies on her bunk, literally beating her head against the concrete wall, wailing from the pain. Finally, she can't even walk. Unable to climb to her top bunk, she lies on mine, crying as I hold her and pray aloud. On June 16th, they finally take her to the hospital while I am at radiation. When I return from treatment, she is gone and the room is painfully silent.

I go to Medical to get my burn cream and pain meds. My chest is a mass of blisters and feels like a tiny fairy is dancing on it with razor blades on the soles of her shoes. The nurse says they don't have my meds and I can buy IBU's at the store. Well, I could if it was Walgreens. We are only allowed to order once a week and I have no money anyway. This is cancer. The meds are ordered. Why can't I get them? Why is everything such a battle?

I am exhausted and worried sick about Gina. I cared for her for weeks, but suddenly I am not allowed to know anything or talk to her parents. "Confidentiality," they say. B.S. That is just the smoke screen they hide behind. The silence is deafening. Gradually, I hear surreptitiously from the guards that Gina has Leukemia and it is serious. But Leukemia is very treatable. I don't understand. Suddenly, two days after they take her to the hospital, Gina is dead. How in the hell does a healthy twenty-five-year-old die so fast? The administration says she had acute Leukemia, fast acting and a death sentence. Does that mean you have to die in misery and pain, isolated and afraid, unable to say goodbye to your children? The shock of Gina's death is overwhelming. There is no counseling for inmates, but they do offer it to the officers. They continue to treat me with ignorance and apathy.

Soon after this, Christine is released, has a second mastectomy, and dies three months later. If her cancer had been diagnosed and treated when she discovered her lump, maybe she'd still be alive too.

Finally, my treatment was over. The radiologist says the protocol is a visit to the oncologist or radiologist alternating every three months for two years, then every six months for two years, and then annually. But this protocol is not followed, and I'm not allowed to see either one. Nine months later, I start the laborious grievance process.

At last, nearly eighteen months after my last visit to the hospital, I am allowed a teleconference with an oncologist who is completely unfamiliar with my case. He answers my questions, but there is no way for him to examine me and he's never seen my file. He recommends a tumor marker test. Six months later, it still hasn't happened. My cancer was stage 3B. My tumor was six centimeters. My margins weren't clean following surgery. At the time, the oncologist said I had a 60% chance to live five years.

Gina and Christine are dead. Those of us with these devastating illnesses feel so totally alone and, for this reason, I start a Cancer Support Group. It took me a year of begging, but I finally got permission. We have fourteen members, all of them with terrifying and heartbreaking stories of neglect.

Before I was indicted, I had normal fears, but I always subscribed to Dr. Susan Jeffer's book, *Feel the Fear and Do It Anyway*. Whatever it was, I could handle it. If it was a problem, I tackled it. A person, I faced them. An event, I met it head on. Sometimes I succeeded. Sometimes I didn't, but always I tried, no matter what . . . except for one fateful time, and that resulted in disaster.

Cancer is a condition to fear, but you can face it. The justice system and prison are another story. Prison with cancer takes fear to a new level. I can control my mind. I can be optimistic. I can pray and believe and have faith, but I know I cannot change the horrible conditions, apathetic nurses, indifferent doctors, and mean-spirited officers. When they make decisions that affect my life, I am helpless. Gina wrote and her family called, but to no avail. They were all helpless.

That is why I am afraid. No amount of platitudes and cute sayings, no mind control, no positive imagery can change the situation. My life and my health are in the hands of the State, and I am helpless against its inadequate, mismanaged, incompetent, apathetic power. This isn't irrational fear about some hostile guard or stupid rule. I can deal with that. This is about the State, an enormous multi-tentacled octopus. Those thousands of tentacles form an impenetrable wall of incompetence. How do I deal with that?

Do you remember the story of Pollyanna? Her father taught her to play the Glad Game. No matter what the circumstances, no matter how afraid or how sad, always look for a reason to be glad. That is really hard in prison, but I decide to play.

- I'm glad I came to prison with cancer because I've experienced something firsthand that most people outside couldn't believe. I can bear witness.

- I'm glad Gina was my roommate and we were able to share her last days together.

- I'm glad my hair loss is visible and makes me vulnerable. As a result, lots of women come to talk to me about the lump they've found or how it felt to lose their mother to cancer. Their stories touch me on so many levels.

- I'm glad Gina's family wants to advocate for changes in the system so that Gina's death will mean something positive.

In the midst of pain, there are reasons to be glad. People are afraid and suffer everywhere. No one's pain is unique, certainly not mine. The first year of this journey was full of pain and not just mine. I had a mastectomy from the jail; Christine had hers from the prison. There were three of us with advanced cancer having chemo and radiation. Christine, Michelle, and I all went together, shackled as a group. They expected Michelle to die or me. Instead Gina died, then Christine. Our pain and our grief were visceral.

But that's just the first year and I know I am going to be here a long time. I have a choice about how to spend it. There's weak and whinny; there's strong and useful. Strong and useful sound better to me. I am not sure how, but somehow I know I am going to take my fear and pain and turn it into power. I'll use the Glad Game to keep my perspective and stay balanced in the darkness. Somehow, I will use this experience to help others survive their pain wherever I go . . . *inside or out.*

Chapter 6

Boobs for Barbie and Dolly

January 2004. After Gina died, everyone was so upset that the administration decided to have a Town Hall Meeting to talk about all the problems in Medical. There was a lot of venting and excuses and promises. I am sorry to say that things didn't change much. However, two things did happen. The new Director attended and we brought to her attention the cruelty of denying fans to inmates in the Arizona heat. At this meeting, she gave the edict that inmates would be allowed to purchase fans from the prison store. That was a huge blessing.

The second thing was very personal. It had been a year since my mastectomy. I'd been told that prostheses are out of the question in prison. Even women with artificial limbs have them taken away upon entry to Perryville. But at this meeting the women spoke up for me. They said it was outrageous that I'd been denied a prosthesis, and it touched a nerve. Later, the policy was reviewed and it was decided that prosthetic breasts would be allowed.

One day soon thereafter, I am called to Medical and measured up, down and around, several times. Nothing is left to chance. Then I am told to do what inmates do best — wait. "Don't call us, we'll call you."

I wait about seven weeks. Finally, I am called back to Medical. I am so excited, I almost fly across the field. When I get there, the nurse opens the precious box to reveal — a boob for Barbie! It is the smallest breast you can imagine, not even close to a 36C. Why in the world did they do all that measuring? My face falls to the floor as the nurse's curves into a scowl, like this is my fault. She gets out the tape measure and measures me up, down and around — several times — again. And again I get the order, "Don't call us, we'll call you." And I wait some more.

About six weeks later, I am again called up to Medical and again I fly across the field. I am so excited — again. With great anticipation the nurse opens the box to reveal — a boob for Dolly Parton! Seriously, it is huge, not even close to what was measured. My face falls — again. And the nurse scowls even deeper.

"We can't keep doing this. These are expensive and they can't be returned" she snaps as my face falls further.

I timidly offer a solution. By that time our Cancer Support Group has started and I know they often provide prosthetics for mastectomy patients. "I can ask our sponsor if they will donate a prosthetic for me." Surprise! It is taken under advisement and, very shortly, it is approved.

Once again I wait, but this time not as long. I am called up to Medical *again* and I fly across the field *again.* I am still excited. We go through the ritual *again.* I hold my breath as she opens the box and then I exhale joyfully. It is perfect! The bras are so pretty; well, not really, but so much better than the State Issue one I've had to wear that just droops on one side.

My posture improves and suddenly I feel so much better. I am standing up straight and tall. A week later I realize that the very painful feeling of a white hot rope burning in my neck is gone. For nearly a year I've had this terrible pain. I thought it was the horrid mattress, but it was the result of being unbalanced. The prosthesis took the pain away. I am so thankful.

I'm also thankful that the ladies spoke up for me at the Town Hall Meeting. That was incredibly kind. Once again, I am struck with the generosity of the women I have met here. Generosity is a wonderful quality to practice wherever you are . . . *inside or out.*

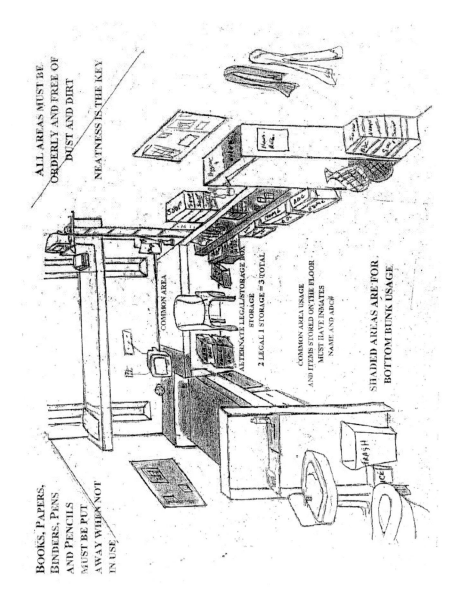

ALL AREAS MUST BE ORDERLY AND FREE OF DUST AND DIRT

NEATNESS IS THE KEY

BOOKS, PAPERS, BINDERS, PENS AND PENCILS MUST BE PUT AWAY WHEN NOT IN USE

COMMON AREA

ALTERNATE LEGAL/STORAGE BOX STORAGE
2 LEGAL 1 STORAGE = 3 TOTAL

COMMON AREA USAGE AND ITEMS STORED ON THE FLOOR MUST HAVE INMATES NAME AND ADC#

SHADED AREAS ARE FOR BOTTOM BUNK USAGE

Chapter 7

Living Conditions: Neatness Counts

February 2003. I recover and I heal, thank God, and I start acclimating to prison life. In prison, neatness counts. There are rules and policies for everything. The Arizona Department of Corrections (ADC) policy manuals take up a complete six-foot shelf in the Deputy Warden's office. Our living area falls under this. Everything has a designated place, and we are provided with a handy diagram so there is no question of proper compliances.I have the bottom bunk so all the shaded areas in the diagram are assigned to me; where I put my toothbrush, my hygiene products, my clock, and my TV (if I had one) are all spelled out. There are places for towels, laundry bags, commissary items, and legal boxes. No creativity allowed.

The room is about six feet by eleven feet. If my roommate and I both need to dress at the same time, it's tight quarters. There is only one chair and it is part of the step-ladder to get up to what I call the Penthouse. Climbing up is really tough. These rooms were built to be singles and then, somewhere along the way, overcrowding demanded double bunking and that has turned out to be hazardous.

First, getting up and down is dicey. The small ladder stands straight up and is designed for gymnasts who are at least 5'6" tall. Gina had no problem. She was young, tall, and thin. She was up and down with the grace of an acrobat. My previous roommate, Mona, was barely five feet tall and weighed about 150 pounds. Her little legs were so short that getting up the ladder for her was almost a miracle. I used to hold my breath. Thank God I have a lower bunk because I'd never make it. Oh, I might get up with some help, but I'm up and down at night going to the bathroom and wrestling with the ladder in the dark would eventually land me on my head.

Storage is another challenge. Each of us is assigned a three foot by three foot drawer for all of our clothes. We don't have much, but it's enough to fill a drawer. We are also allowed three legal boxes for legal papers, books, and mail. This is my downfall. Policy dictates we can own seven books and five magazines. Policy also dictates we can purchase weekly from the store twenty-four pouches of tobacco, ten packs of cigarettes, and seven pouches of chewing tobacco. Per policy, we can smoke ourselves to death, but reading is discouraged. As a non-smoker and voracious reader, this is a problem.

I have a dictionary, a thesaurus, and a Bible. I have books on breast cancer, healing, and inspiration. I treasure them and depend on them as I battle this disease. How can I give those up? Through generous friends, I've received a few magazine subscriptions and I'm borrowing others to read so I'm always over the limit. I can't keep the magazines, but I am keeping articles on nutrition, cancer, exercise, poetry, and money management (an area where I really need help). I set up files for them in my legal box, then learn that policy says we can't tear anything out of a magazine. That makes the magazine contraband. Don't ask me why. I was just trying to be efficient; foiled again by the system.

This tiny room functions as our living room, dining room, bedroom, kitchen, and bathroom. Our bathroom sink is also our kitchen sink because we do cook, but that's another story. So what about the bathroom and privacy? There is none. Any sensitivity you have is left behind with your first strip search. However, I've made up a rule. In our room we have an imaginary door around the toilet. When one of us is on the throne, the door is shut and we have total privacy. We're all pretty considerate and this works very well. I do long for the day when I'll have a real bathroom again but, in the meantime, I have one in my imagination.

"All areas must be free of dust and dirt," says the policy.

That's impossible here, but we try. Perryville sits in a huge dirt-field where dust witches are constantly on attack. Almost daily the wind swirls around us, covering everything in a fine layer of grime. One window is stationary and not designed to open, but the other is supposed to open about three inches for ventilation. It used to open and close but now it's frozen — won't open, won't close. The result is a one-inch crack that everyone tries to seal through various creative efforts. Ours is sealed with Kotex soaked in glue and toothpaste. That works pretty well for about six months, but eventually it starts to shrink and crack and it's back to the drawing board. It does help keep the dust down to a fine powder. I'd hate to think what it would be like without it.

The room is all gray steel and cream concrete. There is no softness. When Gina and I were together, we played a game and decorated the room in our imagination. Of course, money was no object so we mirrored one wall, put down a lovely carpet, painted clouds on the ceiling, and added a hanging basket. Naturally, we wanted comforters and throw pillows and we each got a stuffed teddy bear to hold and pet. We longed for softness and found it in our creativity. Imagination in prison helps us hold on to our sanity.

I don't object to the policies. It saves arguments when roommates aren't as agreeable as Gina and I were. It's the softness and color that I miss, like I miss Gina. And I do agree that neatness does count. It's like living in a shoebox; unfortunately, one from PayLess, not Neiman Marcus. The room feels better when everything is tidy and put away. I actually learned that lesson in my college dorm and it has served me well for forty years. In college or in prison, in a cell or in a castle, it's a good habit to have. Neatness does count . . . *inside or out.*

Chapter 8

Mail Call

March 03. Do you remember when people used to write letters on elegant stationary with matching envelopes? Do you remember cards you could actually hold instead of e-mail ones? Before e-mail, way back even before telephones, letters were magical links between families, friends, and lovers who poured out their emotions on paper. Getting a letter was a special occasion. Remember that movie *The Postman* with Kevin Costner? America had been blown to bits in a vicious war and was ruled by a tyrant whose strength lay in keeping communities and families separated. A small band of postmen on horseback kept the ideas of freedom and democracy alive through the mail. Through that painful separation, mail became a symbol of hope.

Mail Call is an important event in prison. Everyday at 4:15 in the afternoon, our mail is distributed. The C.O. stands at the picnic table in front of our pod and, as the doors open by Central Control, we all come out into the sunshine, blinking at the brightness after the gloomy light of our cells. It would make a great scene in a movie. The vivid orange uniform is in striking contrast to the stark gray walls. Women lounge against the rails upstairs. Downstairs, we sit on concrete benches, trying to look cool and uninterested, like this really isn't very important, when all the while our hearts beat faster as we pray that our name is called.

Some names are called often, almost daily. They are the ones blessed with family and friends who care. Some names are never called. Because they have no one, they rarely leave their bunks for mail call. It is just not worth the effort and the inner humiliation. Every afternoon at 4:15, they are reminded that nobody cares.

That's what a letter is in prison. It's an envelope of hope. It says that in the midst of the outside hustle and bustle, someone has taken the time to stop and acknowledge you as a person. It's a validation of you as a human being, courtesy of the U.S. Mail.

When I entered prison, I didn't expect much mail. I only had one loyal friend and my loving husband. To my surprise, I am immediately provided with a pen pal that I know is a miracle. I met Carolyn when I was in jail, awaiting sentencing. She is a wonderful hairdresser who volunteers to cut hair in the jail as part of her Christian ministry. After chemotherapy I didn't have any hair to cut, but, as I watched her work, we started talking and hit it off. She said she'd write to me in prison and gave me her post office box so I could notify her once I was sentenced. I put the address away without giving it much thought. After all, she didn't know me from Adam's house cat. Why would she write to me?

I'd been in prison about six weeks when suddenly my name is called for mail. I try to nonchalantly stroll over to the C.O. to investigate. My enthusiasm takes over when I see the huge envelope full of treasures. There are stories, jokes, prayers, and news items off the Internet, plus a letter from Carolyn. Since she hadn't heard from me, she looked me up on the Arizona Department of Corrections website (where the ADC inmate database lists all the prison guests) and decided to send me a postal care package. As wordy as I am, there are none to describe my emotions that day. *Joy. Elation. Amazement. Gratitude.* Jail and prison strip you of your self-worth and dignity. We all feel completely valueless as human beings. But, suddenly, Carolyn's spirit reaches out to me across the razor wire and I feel wonderful. I know right away this is a miracle. The chances of my meeting her at the jail were extremely remote, a small window of fate God provided. Carolyn is one of those earthly angels definitely sent to me in a very dark time.

Ironically, the newspaper sends more angels my way. I get a letter out of the blue from a very old friend with whom I'd lost touch years ago. Carmen read our story in the paper and decided to contact me. Another miracle. She called the prison and asked to be connected to my room. There was silence on the other end of the line before the operator said, "Lady, this is a prison, not a Holiday Inn." Then she asked for my e-mail. He laughed. No e-mail in prison, no way. It dawned on Carmen that we're dependent on Pony Express here, and once again I heard my name at mail call.

Little by little, more old friends join the ranks and my name is heard often at mail call. Some even send me priceless magazine subscriptions. *Readers Digest* from Carolyn to lift my spirits. *TIME* magazine from Carmen to help me keep up with the outside world. *VANITY FAIR* from Eleanore to spark my intellectual curiosity. Diane's gift of *Guide Posts* inspires me when I feel blue. Rochelle sends *OPRAH* to encourage my vision. *BAZAAR* from Jane Page fills the room with beauty. Since I have no television, those treasures are my window to the world.

Then Carolyn has a brilliant idea. You know those cards that some magazines provide? You can mail them in requesting brochures and catalogues on travel, fashion, and home living. Well, she sent one in for me and now I get mail almost every day. I get travel and cruise brochures, fashion catalogues, slick glossy ads for beautiful furniture and the latest, hottest cars. It must drive the mailroom crazy, but I don't care. Every day I get to go somewhere dreamy in my imagination and then I pass them on so others can dream too.

The brochures are an unexpected lesson. In my previous life, I would have coveted a lot of what I saw and could not afford. Then I would have been unhappy because, like the rest of America, I thought stuff made you happy. I remember that old bumper sticker "He who dies with the most toys wins." Just like everybody else I wanted the toys. Now I know better. I really enjoy the gorgeous pictures in the ads. They bring color and beauty into a very drab place, but there is nothing I want.

Mail call is a powerful life lesson for me. It reminds me of what is really important in life . . . family, friends, loved ones. Stuff is just stuff. It also reminds me how powerful a letter is and how meaningful it is to receive one behind bars. Postcards, greeting cards, magazine articles, books, magazines. Those cards and letters touch us on many levels, especially the pictures and drawings from children. They open doors to endless possibilities.

Recently, I was stunned to learn that the local Sheriff, who prides himself on being the toughest sheriff in the country, decided to restrict the mail in "his jail." No envelopes are allowed in or out of his facility except legal mail. *Postcards only.* If it can't fit on a postcard, too bad. No more family photos, no drawings by your children, no love letters, no interesting articles. The Sheriff said that sorting the mail was too labor intensive and a security threat, but this approach only adds to the desolation, despair, frustration, and bitterness. Bear in mind that many of these inmates are awaiting trial, haven't had their innocence or guilt established, and can be there for months or even years. They are treated as guilty when the rule of law says innocence is *presumed.* For inmates, it is cruel and unusual punishment and does not contribute to rehabilitation in any way.

Mail is valued in the outside world. Statistics show that less than three percent of our mail now is personal. Ninety-seven percent of the mail we receive is junk or bills. Think of the power of sending a real letter. Think of a person you would like to touch emotionally. If you are reading this book, perhaps you know an inmate. Put the book down and write them a letter instead. Or if you don't know an inmate, just send a card to someone you care about. Not an eCard, a real one. You are sending an envelope of hope and I promise you will touch a life. That is a powerful thing to do . . . *inside or out.*

10 Ways to Be a Pen Pal to an Inmate

1. Get a post office box to insure privacy and convenience.

2. Ask your pastor, priest, or prison volunteer if they know an inmate who would like a pen pal. (Trust me, the list is endless).

3. Decide how many inmates you can write to and decide if you'll write to men, women, or both and the frequency of your packets or letters.

4. Purchase a mail scale so you can determine correct weight and postage. Buy a supply of special edition stamps. Inmates appreciate color.

5. Choose appropriate things for packets. There are pretty pictures of nature and animals from magazines or the Internet. News items, prayers, and inspirational stories are all welcomed and will be shared. Postcards are welcomed too. Everything decorates the bulletin board. (However, some facilities do not allow printouts from the internet. It is always best to check first.)

6. Inmates who have no outside support are often indigent and may ask you for help. Decide how you want to handle this and don't feel guilty if you have to say no. If you do decide to send money, remember even five dollars goes a long way in prison towards necessities. Remember too, prisons only accept money orders. Personal checks won't do. You can get money orders most easily and inexpensively from grocery stores.

7. Inmates aren't allowed perfume so if you spray your letter with perfume, they will love that.

8. Inmates appreciate magazine subscriptions, books, tapes, and/or CDs. These are the only gifts they can receive besides money. Books, tapes, and CDs must be mailed directly from the publisher or bookstore (like Amazon) and all tapes must be in clear plastic cassette holders.

9. Inmates love pretty cards. Forget the ones with music and things like balloons. Those aren't allowed. Just a pretty card is a gift. Clip art and stickers are not allowed either.

10. Long letters aren't critical. Many inmates have not passed mandatory eighth grade education. Find out about your pen pal and keep it simple if necessary. Pictures are welcomed and family life is nice to hear about. You may get long letters or short notes. Just remember, your mail is treasured even if they don't know how to articulate it.

Chapter 9

Spiders and Webs of Deceit

October 2004. Spiders are a big and unpleasant part of prison life in Arizona. It's the desert, it's hot, it's dirty. Spiders love that. No matter how much we clean, they creep into the crevices and crawl through the open doors.

Candace is terrified of spiders and she decides to make our room spider proof. Fine with me. While I don't suffer from arachnophobia, I don't relish one spinning a web over my face while I sleep. So I am all for it, but I wonder how she is going to accomplish this task. We have no access to any kind of bug killers, despite the number of spider bites Medical treats on a weekly basis. But Candace is clever and prison fosters creativity.

First, she stuffs the window cracks with Kotex pads to seal it shut. To do this, you must fill our small plastic bowl (that we are allowed to buy) with water. Then add some of the white paste we are also allowed to buy. Soak the Kotex in the pasty water, then start stuffing the cracks. When the Kotex dries, it's like cement. Good start, but not enough. She needs tape. Inmates are not allowed tape. I have no idea why, but it's another one of those rules.

Candace's creative mind is spinning. She works in the print shop where there are huge rolls of three inch wide packing tape. Perfect. But how will she bring it back to our room? The women in the print shop are strip-searched everyday after work. There is no way to smuggle a paper clip and certainly not tape. But everyday, little by little, Candace seals our window with packing tape. How in the world? The best way — *hide in plain sight*. Everyday she wraps about a foot of tape around the name-tag we all must wear prominently on our orange shirts. The tape is clear and no one notices. Mission accomplished. The window cracks are all sealed up with Kotex and pilfered tape. No spiders are sneaking through that window.

Except that the next day, Candace finds a web at the head of my cot. No spider, just a web. I clean it off and forget about it. Then she finds another web twice as big at the head of her cot. That little sucker is industrious. I clean this web off too and I grease the window sash with hair grease sprinkled with the nasty smelling foot powder we can buy from the ADC store. Just the smell should discourage any self-respecting bug. But later she sees the actual spider and screams. I put down the letter I am writing to investigate.

That isn't easy. First, I have to climb up on her cot. Small, tiny ladder. Very high cot. Candace spots me so I don't fall. After all, I'm no longer a spring chicken. Once up in the penthouse, I aim her light at the window sash and, lo and behold, I do see long black spider legs and a large spider body in the V of the sash. We have nothing to kill spiders. First, I try hair spray, but it has no alcohol in it and he just curls up and retreats out of my reach. Perched on the upper bunk, I look around our tiny room for potential weapons. Shampoo? Hand lotion? Ginger Ale? Pickin's are slim and Candace is frantic.

"What do we need?" she cries.

"I need some RAID!" I wail.

Oh, hell, I think, *what in the world can I do?* This is serious. Black widows and brown recluses are prevalent in the desert.

"Ok," I say, "Boil some water."

She jumps to it with great enthusiasm because she hates spiders and is ready to spend the night on the floor. How to boil water in prison with no stove? All we have is one of those immersion heater coils that we call a *stinger*. With it we boil water for coffee, heat soup, melt cheese, make icing with cocoa, and steam our faces for a facial. Where there's a will, there's a way.

While Candace is boiling the water, I watch the spider to make sure he doesn't escape. When the water is ready, she clears off the window ledge and places our plastic bowl there. She blesses the water like Holy Water and passes the cup to me. As I begin to pour the boiling water over the window sash, I say a prayer and hold my breath, secretly afraid the spider is laying in wait to spring out at me.

Success! The hot water washes the spider out and he free-falls perfectly into the waiting bowl with nary a splash. From my perch, I see his feeble attempt to swim.

"Quick, Candace, flush it!" I shout.

But Candace, who can jog three miles in 110-degree heat and leap tall buildings in a single bound, is paralyzed.

"No! No!" She yells, "I can't look. I can't touch it."

Very carefully, I climb down and retrieve the bowl to examine my prey. It is indeed a big, black and nasty looking spider that is now going to a watery grave.

Candace says I'm her hero and I do my triumphant spider dance, the Spider Shuffle. I'd still prefer Raid. Even the officers aren't allowed to have bug spray. I have no idea why, but it leaves us all vulnerable and there are way too many bites.

What did I learn from all of this? I learned that Candace and I are a pretty good team, boiling water has many uses, and a little prayer before battle is a good thing . . . *inside or out.*

Chapter 10

Date Night

January 2004. Years ago, when David and I started our own business, it seemed like every waking hour was devoted to it. All we did was talk shop. Like a relentless PAC-MAN, it gobbled up our every thought and action. As months went by, we realized our conversations, our thoughts, and our relationship all were suffering. Grumpy and short-tempered, we weren't laughing much anymore.

Then I suggested *Date Night.* Once a week, we would dedicate an evening to us, to enjoy dinner and a movie, a long walk, a concert — something to distract us from work so that we could focus on each other. And no business allowed. No marketing, no design ideas, and no pesky math. At first it was surprisingly hard; we were so focused on work. Gradually, however, it got easier to remember how to talk about books and movies, art and music, gardening and cooking and travel, all those things we'd temporarily forgotten. We discovered each other again and remembered why we fell in love. Date Night became an essential element in our week. It refreshed and strengthened our relationship.

Then we went to different prisons — together. The separation was overwhelming and painful. After seventeen years of marriage, suddenly we were apart. As inmates, we couldn't even write to each other immediately. Married couples in prison must prove they are legally married before they are allowed to correspond. A blessed friend had to locate our marriage license.

Meanwhile, we piggy-backed. That is the highly illegal prison practice of sending a letter to a friend or middleman who then forwards it on. And woe to anyone who is caught. You can lose your mail privileges, a disaster in prison. Fortunately, we didn't have to do that for long before our marriage license was retrieved and we were approved. It was a huge relief, because at that time I was going through all of the cancer treatments. David was desperately worried about me and I longed to reach out to him. Hearing his voice on paper was healing for both of us.

Suddenly more restrictions pop up. Inmates corresponding with other inmates are not allowed to exchange greeting cards or even clippings from a newspaper. We can't exchange photographs either. Even at Christmas time, correspondence only, anything else is contraband. Prisons aren't about relationships; prisons are about separation. Yet I am stunned to learn just how many families there are in prison. On my yard there are wives, mothers and daughters, aunts and cousins. Conversely there are husbands, fathers and sons, uncles and nephews in the men's prisons. There is a lot of piggy-backing going on.

This is a national tragedy that perpetuates itself. Family members like David and me are restricted to two fifteen-minute phone calls a year, one in July and one in December. How I look forward to that. The sound of his voice resonates in my brain for weeks afterwards. What do we talk about? Nothing important. It's just lovely to feel so close. Some prison systems allow more phone calls and even visits between spouses and family members to encourage the family unit, but not in Arizona.

About ten months into this experience, I started thinking of something that could bring us closer together under such restrictions. Then I remembered my friend Phyllis. She was married to a Navy pilot who was shot down over Hanoi during the Vietnam war. He was in prison seven long years and there was no communication. It was a living nightmare. About three years after he was shot down, I asked Phyllis how she kept her sanity. She said she scheduled something important every month, a concert, a special visit with friends, a weekend trip. She created something to look forward to every month to ease the pain of the separation. It was her very own type of Date Night.

I decide we need to revive Date Night for us. But how do we do that in prison? Well, our wedding anniversary is January 31st, so we decide we will have our date on the last night of each month. Instead of dinner and a movie, we will write a special date letter on a subject of our choosing and at exactly 8:30 in the evening, after lockdown, we will open our letters and create a mental link in time.

At first, we write random things. I even create a crossword puzzle, and that's not easy. I have a new respect for the people who make those. Then one day I open Pandora's box. I ask David to tell me about his childhood and how he learned to fly. David protested. He's not really a writer and it was so long ago, but then he sat down to write and his first chapter blew me away.

He started writing about a much simpler time and his reminiscences took me back to 1944 in Ocean City, Maryland. It was a small community where everyone knew everyone else, where children were safe to explore and have adventures without fear of danger. When he described his grandmother's home-cooking, my mouth watered. When he took his first flight, my heart beat faster, reliving the exhilaration through his words.

Every month I get a new chapter about the summer of '44, when David started his love affair with flying. He even titled it *A Love Affair*. Every month he sits down to write a new chapter of that most formative time of his life and he says the memories return easier than he expected. The characters of his youth come alive again and provide us both with a mental escape to a gentler time. As the story unfolds, I await our Date Night with great anticipation and delight.

What do I write in return? I write these, my essays about my prison journey. From these, David gets to know the revolving cast of characters who inhabit my world. These give me a chance to poke fun at the system and remind me of my blessings. They are my version of a journal.

Through these date letters, we learn more about each other and ourselves. Prison allows us to develop another dimension in our relationship for which we're grateful. However, we both look forward to Date Nights when we can at last hold hands again and look into each other's eyes. We plan to continue the tradition for the rest of our lives.

Recently I was talking to a friend who said she and her husband had gotten so busy they had started neglecting each other. It's a common occurrence in what I call the real world. I told her about Date Night and she suggested it to her husband. There was a moment of stunned silence before he said, "Who are you and what have you done with my wife?" He was delighted with her suggestion and they scheduled their own Date Night, which turned out to be a huge success. I often feel useless in here and it was nice to know my idea was a catalyst for them.

Relationships, good, strong relationships, don't just happen. They take work — awareness, sensitivity, and a conscious effort. In prison, David and I have to work harder, but we are much more conscious of what we are missing. We know we will never again be quick to take the simple daily pleasures for granted as we did in that previous life. If I do, David has permission to shoot me at dawn. Just kidding, neither of us wants to get up that early. In prison, we rekindle all those precious memories: working in the garden, cooking with the fresh harvest of our garden, walking the dogs, sharing an ice cream cone, just holding hands. I never think much about the charity balls and dress-up occasions. It's the simple pleasures I treasure . . . *inside and out.*

Chapter 11

The Birthday Party

July 2004. The invitations are individual works of art: small, appliquéd American flags of red, white, and blue. The picnic tables are set in the shade of the tree and decorated with flowers of mauve, pink, and yellow. The guests are fashionably dressed in varying shades of the year's hottest color, orange. It sounds trés chic, but the flags are made of construction paper and glue, the metal tables are under the lone tree on the gray prison yard, and the orange is the ugly uniform of an inmate.

A party in prison? Yes, they happen, mostly for birthdays, and this one is for three of us, Melissa, Candace, and me — all July babies. Because we all have different friends, not all the guests know each other so I decide on a game, my old favorite, *Get Acquainted Bingo.* I have painstakingly drawn twenty bingo cards with grids (recreated below) and have my treasured colored pencils ready to distribute to each guest. The object of the game is to get each square signed by a different person until the entire sheet is signed — a Bingo blackout. It forces you to circulate and talk to everyone. The descriptions should be tailored to your guest list.

Frankly, I'm a bit nervous as I distribute the cards and give instructions. Will these women be too cool for a silly game? I have successfully played this from Phoenix to Portugal with ages from eight to eighty, but this is a different audience. As they look at the cards, there is complete silence while I hold my breath. Suddenly, almost in unison, they jump up and start darting around getting the coveted signatures. They are talking and laughing, actually mixing just like in real life. Finally, we hear "BINGO!" The proud winner is Lisa, a darling young woman who has served fourteen years of a sixteen-year sentence. She wins a bottle of *DOM Perryville:* a very young vintage of Ginger Ale that Candace has decorated with a Champagne label.

Time for the appetizers. Potluck is a tradition in prison. Everyone brings a dish to show off her culinary skills, a huge challenge here. Inmates are allowed to buy a very limited array of food items from the company store. Almost everything available is junk. Lots of chips and candy, but only three items of protein: peanut butter, tuna, and beans. These make up the bulk of our menus. What can you do with junk food? The creations are amazingly good, but ultra high in carbs and calories.

Val's hors d'oeuvres are a hit. She made cheesy tuna roll-ups — tuna, mayonnaise, cheese, and jalapenos rolled up in tortillas. She cut them into bite size pieces using our cutting tool, the edge of our very small plastic mirror. No knives allowed. Val even made a serving tray by painting and decorating the bottom of the box that brownies come in, lining it with a pretty magazine ad. Not exactly hygienic, but certainly pretty. The roll-ups are served with a tasty sauce made from squeeze cheese, mayonnaise, and powdered milk. No seasoning allowed, but somehow inmates find a way.

Candace made a yummy sour cream and onion cheese dip. Take a bag of Sour Cream and Onion Potato Chips and crush them to a fine texture. (Keep them in the bag and use a water bottle as your rolling pin.) Using the bag as your mixing bowl, add three packages of squeeze cheese, powdered milk and jalapeno juice to taste. Consistency should be creamy. Serve in a bowl with tortillas or crackers. Don't ask about the calories.

For the main course, the tables are set with our beautiful prison china, white plastic bowls filled with various delicacies. We're only allowed one small bowl so cooking is a challenge. Most inmates actually have two bowls, but the second one is contraband and on quarterly shakes, the C.O.'s routinely throw it away. So then everyone buys a new one for twenty-five cents. It gives the company store more business and inmates then have two bowls for the next three months. It's a prison game everyone plays.

The highlights of the main course are creatively called *Pasta with Tuna* and *Sour Cream Chicken*. (Recipes included). Do not consider making these unless you are rail thin, have ridiculously low cholesterol, and just love junk food, because it is indeed junk food.

After we've eaten much more than our stomachs are used to, desserts are forthcoming. Kristy has dazzled us with a delicious chocolate cake made from candy bars. I made chocolate mint truffles, lots of work, but well worth it; easy to serve and bite size. I too decorated a brownie box for serving. In an ugly place, we appreciate the efforts to make things pretty.

Finally, comes the *piéce de résistance* — Melissa's lemon birthday cake, star shaped, and decorated with stars. Melissa was sick the week before the party and, for a few privileged days, she got meals in her room when dessert was lemon pudding. She carefully saved it for icing and filling. The cake itself was a mix of *Vanilla Zingers* and *Dunkin' Sticks* layered with the lemon filling. She laboriously worked it into the shape of a star, then iced it all with a mixture of pudding, milk, and lemon drops melted in hot water. The extra stars were made by rolling Star Bursts flat with a water bottle (yes, it takes forever) and then using our special mirror cutting tool to cut the star shapes. The effort is intense, but they really look fantastic, shiny, colorful, and sparkly. It is the most beautiful cake I've seen in prison, and we dub Melissa the Martha Stewart of Perryville.

Of course, no birthday party would be complete without singing and presents. The singing is enthusiastic and the presents very special, all handmade, except for mine. I have a very significant milestone. The girls give me rollers and mascara this year. Last year, I had lost all of my hair and eye lashes to chemotherapy and was painfully bald. This year I have a little bit of hair to roll. I am thankful.

As the sky turns all the gorgeous sunset hues of the Arizona desert (despite the razor wire fences, we can still see the sky), the party talk mellows to past birthdays in prison and out. Melissa hit twenty-eight; Candace is forty; and I am one year short of sixty. The hardest milestone is Candace's. Turning forty in prison is not exactly reason to celebrate. She is due for release in three weeks and fears starting over with nothing. But I know that with her energy and drive, she'll be on top again in no time. Melissa fears she is losing her youth and the best years of her life, but she is beautiful with a perfect figure and an excellent mind. I know her best years are in front of her.

From the prospective of our ages, our fears are different. Because I've lost everything and am essentially homeless, I fear being a bag lady, sleeping under a bridge somewhere, but then I stop, knowing that's ridiculous. I am blessed with a brain, energy, enthusiasm, friends, faith, and David. I know I will not be under a bridge.

It is a wonderful day to celebrate and practice the little niceties of life. We are isolated in such an ugly place, but we use our creative energy to produce a pretty party to share with our friends. It's the closest thing possible to normal behind the razor wire. It lifts our spirits and brings laughter into our lives. No matter where you are or what your circumstance, remember that you are a creative spirit with much to contribute and share. Sharing that creativity and joy will give meaning to your life . . . *inside or out.*

BELIEVE IT OR NOT RECIPES
These are Surprisingly Delicious and Completely BAD for You

Sour Cream & Onion Chicken

2 Bowls
Small amount of milk (pilfered from somewhere)
2 pouches of chicken in gravy (mostly gravy)
1 bag Sour Cream & Onion Potato Chips (finely crush chips
in the bag using a water bottle)
Grilled potatoes pilfered from breakfast
Chopped Jalapeños

Boil 1 cup of water with a stinger. Pour into bowl, and
immerse pouch of chicken & gravy. Heat up about 3 minutes.

Pour 1 bag crushed chips in 2nd bowl. Add warm chicken and
mix well.

Add some potatoes and keep mixing. Add chopped jalapeños
to taste and some milk to smooth consistency.

Repeat with the 2nd pouch.

When it's all mixed well, combine the bowls. Then wash out the
empty bowl and line with Saran Wrap. Add all the mixture to this
bowl, pressing tightly to make a mound.

Turn out on a serving box you've decorated with pretty magazine ads
and covered with Saran Wrap you've pilfered from somewhere. Decorate the mound with whole chips and surround it with crackers.

Alternatively, you can roll it up in tortillas and serve.

Pasta with Tuna

1 Ramen Vegetable Noodle Soup
1 Tuna pouch
1 bag Sour Cream Chips (crush chips by using a water bottle)
1 Squeeze Cheese Packet

3 Mayonnaise Packs
Whole or Chopped Jalapeños (to taste)
Salt & Pepper (pilfered)

Boil water and add to soup to cover noodles/pasta. Let sit until all the water is absorbed with the pasta.
In a bowl, mix well Tuna, 1 cheese pack, 3 mayonnaise packs, salt & pepper.

In another bowl, mix crushed chips with one pack cheese and a little hot water. Mix so it looks like cheese chunks. Then mix it all together with the tuna.

Add Jalapeños to taste. Serve with crackers.

Chocolate Mint Truffles

6 Brownies, mashed in a bowl
4 Dunkin Sticks, well crushed in a bowl
6 Peppermints, finely crushed
2 pats of butter with melted cocoa to taste. (You have to sneak the butter off your breakfast tray. If caught, it's a major ticket for stealing from your own tray.)

Mix brownies in a bowl to a consistency of fudge.
Mix Dunkin Sticks to a doughy texture in another bowl. Combine and add melted butter. Texture should be like fudge. Add cocoa to taste.

To crush peppermints, throw them, wrapped in paper, very hard on the floor. Roll crushed bits with a water bottle to crush more. Take out the big bits and eat them! Then add the crushed bits to the truffle mix and mix well. Roll out truffles to the size of small cherry tomatoes. Sprinkle with cocoa powder.

Chill and serve on a brownie box you've painted and lined with pretty magazine paper, covered with cling film (also pilfered from someone's sack lunch.)

Get Acquainted Bingo

Has read Gone with the Wind	Loves Cats	Loves to Dance	Has been to New York
Has Voted	Doesn't Smoke	Works Out Regularly	Loves to Cook
Has been to Mexico	Has Blue Eyes	Loves Dogs	Has a GED

Chapter 12

Language

September 2004. Have you listened lately to how people speak our language? I don't mean what Katie Couric says on the nightly news. I mean what your neighbor, your spouse, your teenager, or the kids next door are saying. Sometime in the last century, not so long ago, the F word was considered really, really bad, truly the worst obscenity in our vocabulary. If you said that, people knew you were serious. How times have changed.

Remember *Gone with the Wind?* When Scarlett O'Hara Butler realizes her husband Rhett Butler is leaving her, she cries out to him in anguish, "Where shall I go? What shall I do?"

As he puts on his fantastic Panama hat, he looks straight at her and says, "Frankly, my dear, I don't give a damn."

Millions read these lines in the best-selling novel, but Hollywood had a fierce battle with the censors to allow *damn* in the movie. Until then, damn simply wasn't heard on the silver screen. Once damn was uttered, Pandora's Box was opened and anything was possible. Of course, that was in 1939. It took about thirty-five years to allow the F word. I think M*A*S*H started it, and now it's almost a miracle to see a movie without it.

Walk along the street, stand in a line at the supermarket, or visit a schoolyard. You'll be stunned. It's not used for emphasis in dramatic situations; it's become a ubiquitous verb, adverb, and adjective. Half the words in a sentence can start with F.

We seem to be numb to it. No one really hears it anymore. But the children hear it. They hear it in the movies, in the kitchen, in the car, and in the living room. The movies and television are full of it; bad language and bad attitude. *Two and a Half Men* is training a little wise guy. *The Simpsons* is a lesson in how to insult people. The list is endless and sarcasm wins the day, always at someone's expense. It's one thing for adults to watch, aware that this behavior isn't acceptable at the office. It's another for kids to watch and think it's cool. They hear and they copy — to be like the big kids, like mom and dad, like the movie stars. We're creating another generation of foul-mouthed, sarcastic, negative people.

I used to swear back when it was still shocking and I did it for shock value. It was very effective. Then I lived in Europe and one day a Swedish friend asked me why our movies were so full of vulgar language. I said that it was our culture and very common in the United States. Embarrassed at how bad we looked as a nation, I began to clean up my act.

Then my eyes were really opened. I came to prison where the language simply left me speechless. There are so many young women who cannot speak without using this word. Honestly, if we made it impossible to use, I think they'd all be mute. It's become as common as a "fucking coke" and "fucking fries." And it's extremely limiting. The only way they know how to insult each other is with this basic four letter word.

"Fuck you."

"No, fuck you."

"I fucking said fuck you, bitch."

They throw it back and forth like a ping-pong ball and it would be really comical if it weren't so sad. The truth is we have created a monster of *free speech.* And what is free about it? In the long run, it's very expensive. It costs us our manners, our civility, our vocabulary, our creativity, and our love. If we are throwing vulgarities at each other like big clods of dirt, we have no time to be gentle, kind, and loving. The words sound aggressive and they are.

I like words like puppy and tapioca; they make me smile. Words like daffodil and sunshine fill me with light. Words like love and hope fill me with joy. Using happy, positive, optimistic words can become just as much a habit as nasty, negative ones.

So I decided to stop swearing completely and I practice using happy words. Surprisingly, my language seems to impact others and I notice less swearing in my vicinity. (Or is it my age?) Whatever it is, I appreciate that my behavior acts as a positive influence and that inspires me to keep it up. Everything in life requires practice so my practice might as well be positive, a good habit to maintain . . . *inside and out.*

Chapter 13

Pizza and Sunshine

October 04. Four days and a wake up. Three days and a wake up. Two days and a wake up. The count down began three weeks earlier when the announcement shook the yard. Inmates will be allowed to buy pizza for charity. Pizza Hut will sell the prison large pizzas for $6. The prison will add a $4 contribution for Special Olympics. For $10, we will get Pizza Hut delivered to our prison door, all for charity.

This tantalizing possibility has been dangled before us for over a year. Last year an inmate committee was appointed and they took orders for 1400 pizzas. Anticipation soared, then all hopes were shattered. The accounting department said it would be too much work, and the catering service concession said they would lose money because no one would eat in the cafeteria. To a chorus of I told-you-so's, cynicism prevailed. So when this new announcement came, we exercised cautious optimism, placed our orders, and began the countdown.

Nothing in prison is easy. The logistics of this exercise require endless meetings, false starts, changes, and many nay-sayers.

"Inmates don't deserve anything special."

"We're too short staffed."

"The bookkeeping will be a nightmare."

"We can't maintain security and there will be a riot over the pizza."

Each argument was gradually overcome with the overriding cry: "It's for charity."

The inmate committee took the orders for cheese or pepperoni. Each inmate account had to be checked and double checked to make sure there was indeed enough money in the account to cover the expenditure. Lists were counted and recounted because inmates are constantly being moved to other yards or back to court. Nothing was left to chance. And up until the last minute, we held our breath, knowing they could still change their mind. We breathed easier when we heard the check had actually been sent to Pizza Hut. Hope sprang out all over again.

Finally the big day arrives, bright and clear, actually just another of our endless Saturdays. Breakfast at seven, girls working out, playing cards, doing laundry, and getting ready for much anticipated visits. All ears, however, are focused on the radio chatter. At nine a cheer goes up when we hear that the *ADW has gone to the front gate to receive the pizza delivery trucks.*

We patiently wait until 10:30 when the order comes. *Lock it down.* Never have we moved so quickly to our rooms, happy to slam those doors and wait some more. Finally through the narrow window, I can see the truck drive up, followed by inmates carrying tables and chairs, trailed by the supervisory staff. Soon the tables are piled high with pizza boxes. Pod by pod, the doors are unlocked and women line up to receive their boxes and be checked off. Meg generously bought pizza for both of us, one cheese and one pepperoni. She also bought one for Sally who, like me, is not exactly rolling in dough, pizza or otherwise.

Back in our room, the door slams shut for eleven o'clock count, and Meg and I are alone with fresh, hot pizza. We are giddy with excitement. First, we examine the boxes, appreciating the bright red color in our drab little room. We actually read all the copy before opening the box to marvel at the beautiful pizza so artistically arranged. Actually, it's just normal pizza cut into normal slices like we've all eaten hundreds of times outside. But we aren't outside, and for many, it's been years since they have seen Pizza Hut. For Eva, it's been eleven years, for Cindy, sixteen, for Mary, twenty years. Try to imagine that.

The rich, saucy, cheesy smell fills our tiny room as we make a momentous decision — pepperoni first. Never has a pizza tasted so good. We chew slowly, savoring each bite, dissecting the individual flavors: real tomatoes, real cheese, and real pepperoni. In between chewing, we giggle, we laugh, we jump up and down. I'm not sure why we feel such joy, but it is heady and infectious. It is partly the pizza. It is scrumptious. But it is also the joy of having such a special treat, such an unprecedented, previously forbidden event behind bars.

At noon, the doors open and Meg and I prepare for a little al fresco picnic in the warm autumn sun. But there are more treats in store. We all look at each other in stunned silence when we hear the announcement, "All yards are open for one hour." The four Santa Cruz yards are kept separated through a convoluted system of scheduling so this is unheard of. (This unprecedented treat comes from our Deputy Warden, Ms. Bailey, who always sees inmates as human beings and is an optimist at heart.) It takes a few minutes for the news to sink in, but gradually we head for the gates and the main recreation field. Everyone is out laughing, jogging, sharing pizza, and visiting with friends. We are very grateful for this surprising treat and for the Deputy Warden's faith in us.

I stroll with Meg and Sally, then stop to see Gale and Debra. The giddiness continues over such luxuries. It's rather like a street fair without the hippy artists and food booths. I want to actually sit on the grass, so I walk to the middle of the field and sink down in the greenest spot I can find. (Remember this is Arizona, so it's not exactly lush.) I'm hoping for softness, but fat chance. It is actually very prickly, with lots of busy ants. I don't care. I lean back to soak up the soft sunlight and watch the parade. The women, bright orange Halloween pumpkins, laugh and chatter while the guards in their drab brown uniforms stand silently, eyes moving, watching for the slightest hint of trouble.Of course, there is none. We all know that one tiny misstep can shut this down and ruin any future possibilities. Anyone who dares act up will incur the wrath of the entire inmate population. But all is calm and all is very bright. We are simply too full of pizza and joy to act up.

Besides the $4,000 raised for Special Olympics, there was more generosity. There are many inmates who are indigent, without family support, and even if they're lucky enough to have a job, it only pays ten cents an hour. There was no way they could afford pizza. But inmates like Meg and Lisa and Jeri and Melissa and all the others too numerous to name bought extra pizza to give away. No one went hungry on this special day. Sharing is a big thing inside. Nobody has much, but what they do have is shared. I've seen more generosity inside from criminals with nothing than I ever saw outside from people who have everything. Why is that? I think it comes from pain and heartbreak. When you really suffer, something transformational can happen. You realize you don't want anyone to hurt the way you have. So your compassion increases and with compassion comes generosity.

One lovely day in October in prison, all hearts were mended, full of love and joy over something so simple, so abundant outside, pizza and sunshine. The next time you have pizza, think about how you can share something of yourself with the rest of the world. There are many ways to share and many hearts that need mending. If women in prison with nothing can find something to share, so can you. I know your generosity can make a difference . . . *inside or out.*

Chapter 14

The Book Fair

November 2004. Prison is a microcosm of a town with every personality, every emotion, every drama possible, all enacted under the watchful supervision of our keepers. It's a little bit like that ultimate reality movie *The Truman Show* where Jim Carrey's every action is being recorded. I'm usually pretty good at staying out of the drama because so much of it involves relationships, but suddenly I find myself swirling in the midst of one and I should have known better.

I've had three glorious days. Mrs. K., our librarian, got approval to hold a Book Fair benefiting Crisis Nursery. The plan is to work with Scholastic Books. They will bring in bookshelves on wheels stocked with colorful displays of books, games, posters, toys, and stuffed animals like *Cat in the Hat* and *Clifford, The Big Red Dog*. The women will have an opportunity to buy Christmas gifts for their children and they are giddy with excitement. This is a first in an Arizona prison. It is the closest thing to a real shop some of them have seen in years with really lovely things to buy, and it is a fantastic way to reach out to their children.

The Chaplain, my boss, is in the hospital so I volunteer to help out. It becomes one of the best experiences of my prison journey. It is almost like working in a real store, albeit one where the customers are a bit like locusts, frantic to grab everything, terrified it may vanish before their eyes like a mirage. I love helping the ladies make just the right selections for their children, imagining their smiles and excitement. It is so much fun. And at night, I fall onto my cot with a welcomed exhaustion, happy to have been useful and of service.

Then my bubble bursts. Mrs. K. calls me out to say the ADW had received a desk full of kites about me, complaining that I am helping my friends get special merchandise. Well, it's partly true.

I am helping, but "friends" is a stretch. The truth is I have so few friends here. I am helping basically anyone who asks me, mostly the women who work at the one job on the yard that pays minimum wage. Because they have the most money to spend, they also are the most sensitive about who is getting the best service. I'm damned if I do and damned if I don't. Obviously somebody with a jealous bone complained because they didn't get the attention someone else got. But I love customer service and I love helping people, so I'm doing what comes naturally. Outside, I'd get a commendation from my boss. Inside, I am sent back to my room while she sorts it out.

A few hours later I am back in the library. Mrs. K. decides I can go back to work. She understands the extreme insecurity and neediness that exists in prison and she knows how hard I am working. I don't feel good about the injustice of it all. However, I do recognize where I am and it gives me pause to consider my actions. I apologize to Mrs. K. I am sorry she had to deal with such pettiness in the middle of a frantic week. I told her the truth. I helped anyone who asked me. I even worked with two of Gina's friends who bought marvelous gifts for all her children, choosing just the perfect books and toys for each of them. I was definitely guilty. Isn't it funny how inside, I am chastised for my enthusiasm whereas outside it's a plus?

This whole thing is upsetting. I am so careful here to conduct myself properly. My favorite quote by St. Francis is: "Preach well today, my brothers, even if you must speak." I try to follow that. I'm certainly not an evangelist and I never preach, but I do try to be kind to everyone. Sometimes that is a real challenge — when an officer talks to you like you are the scum of the earth, or inmates drop kites on you for helping. Sometimes I get discouraged. Thank God for optimism and hope. They keep me focused and balanced in an unbalanced place.

Finally, when the last customer is rung up and the last book packed away, the total sales amount to over $15,000 with 30% of that going to the Crisis Nursery. Mrs. K. is ecstatic and I imagine Scholastic Books is too. This may be the first ever book fair in a prison, but I don't think it will be the last. It was such a positive experience for everyone. Yes, I had a little kick in the shins, but even that didn't dampen my enthusiasm for the event.

For a second, I considered becoming a low profile inmate who doesn't get involved in things. That way I'd never be criticized and I'd stay off the staff radar, but that is ridiculous. That would be giving up my joy and letting negativity win. Bad idea.

Instead, I bless the situation and look for reasons to "Count it all joy." Sometimes things just stink and finding any joy is hard, but I'm convinced there is always a broader picture we just can't see. I guess it's for what I can't see sometimes that I'm thankful. It's that knowing inside that everything will be all right, even though I can't see how. It's that ultimate trust I have in my heart for which I am extremely grateful . . . *inside and out.*

> *Everything will be alright in the end.*
> *If it's not alright, it's not the end.*
> Anonymous

Chapter 15

Christmas

December 2004. I am surprised how quickly Autumn passes. Suddenly it's Christmas, the best Christmas I've had in prison and I feel very blessed. I remember my first Christmas in Perryville in 2002. I was so thankful to be out of Estrella, that horror of a place. Admitted to Perryville on December 12th, I was in R&A (Reception & Assessment). It was bleak, but any place was better than Estrella. I was grateful for three hot meals a day, the feeling of the sun on my face, and a breeze, real air, not the stale jail air that never changed. I was determined to honor the holiday and the spirit of Christmas.

On Christmas Eve after dinner, my roommate Tiffany and I began our modest celebration. With a Bible smuggled to us by an old number (an inmate who has been here a long time), I read the Christmas story from Luke. We sang the carols we knew and I read some little inspirational stories, also smuggled to us. Why were these forbidden in R & A? I don't know, but we treasured them. We had no decorations or Christmas cards. We had no gifts to exchange. We did have faith and love and I know the spirit of Christmas was there in our tiny cell.

In 2003, Melissa and I celebrated together. Gina had died in June and we keenly felt her loss. We also heard that Christine's treatment was not working. She was dying. It was a sad time, but we were determined to celebrate life as I knew they would have wanted. I decorated my bulletin board with pictures of Christmas trees and wreaths carefully saved from magazines. It looked so festive and colorful that even the C.O.'s approved, although inmates aren't supposed to decorate their bulletin boards with pictures torn from magazines. In prison, everything must be used for its original purpose or it becomes contraband. A torn-out magazine page becomes contraband because its intended purpose is to be a page in the magazine. Don't even think of being creative. At sunset, some of us were called up to pill call for our weekly meds. It was actually a pleasant stroll across the yard to the administration area and as I looked up at all the razor wire swirled across the tops of the gray buildings, the setting sun reflected on it causing the silver to twinkle like Christmas lights. For an instant, I was transported in my imagination to a place of beauty. Razor wire is such a nasty, vicious, cruel thing, but the sunset transformed it and made it sparkle.

I got my pills and, just as I passed the Programs Office, I noticed a tiny, lighted Christmas tree perched on the top of a filing cabinet shining out of the darkness. It had been two years since I saw a lighted Christmas tree and this little one was such a blessing. It brought back memories of all the Christmas trees in my past. Our tree was always filled with ornaments I'd collected over the years from around the world, each ornament a cherished memory. I closed my eyes and remembered it in my imagination.

In 2003, Melissa and I continued the tradition; we read the story in Luke and shared memories of Christmases past. That year we had a Christmas Eve service brought to prison by our loyal and compassionate priest, Father Knott. We sang all the old familiar carols, had communion, and enjoyed a feeling of indescribable peace. I knew once again that the spirit of Christmas was there.

In 2004, joy starts on December 23rd at 3:13 in the afternoon with my semi-annual phone call with David. Oh, the sheer pleasure of hearing his voice. So much to say in the allotted fifteen minutes. All my thoughts go out the window and all I can say is *I love you, I love you,* while we laugh and cry at the same time. The clock on the wall tick tocks and we talk of our health, our jobs, our hopes, and our love. My C.O. allows two precious extra minutes, but even seventeen minutes flies by and then it is over until July. Never mind, I fly back to the yard on the wings of his voice, my face glowing with joy.

The glow continues. At night, we attend church. Barbara, our dedicated volunteer, brings red silk poinsettias and a small crèche to decorate her snowy white cloth on our make-shift altar. She brings her CD player with a lovely variety of Christmas music. We sing and pray, happy to be together in faith. At the end of the service, when she blows out the dark red candles, we all stand around sniffing the familiar smell of burnt wax, an aroma that brings back memories of Christmas past.

Christmas Eve is a clear, bright day and I have a mission. I volunteered to help our art department (Debra, Mary, and Gale) paint Christmas decorations on the windows of our cafeteria. We start at eleven o'clock, singing carols loudly and off-key, laughing and just happy to be together with such a creative project. I can't draw stick figures, but I can follow a template and I can color within the lines. I happily draw circles of various sizes for Mary to fill with colorful Christmas characters while Debra paints pine branches and wreaths.

When the circles are drawn, I graduate to painting Christmas balls high up on the windows. I gain a new respect for Michelangelo. How in the world did he survive so many years creating the Sistine Chapel? I am tired just reaching up painting for a few hours. Nevertheless, it is a happy tired. Artists really do live in the moment. Right now I am only concerned with the circles and the colors. There is no time to fret or focus on past problems or future what-ifs.

Later, back at our bungalow, Meg and I put the finishing touches on our Christmas gifts. I prepare a little dip for our Christmas Eve get-together and line the top of my legal box with cheerful green paper to create my tray. The doors all grind open at five in the evening. and with the tray loaded, I rush out to save the table under our one tree, a perfect setting for our Christmas celebration.

It is approaching twilight as we start. I ask Kristy, Meg, and Kirsten to follow my tradition and read from the book of Luke. The familiar words bring a sense of calmness to our little group. Then I read a very short story about love and forgiveness and we go around the table saying what we are thankful for this year. Family and friends win the day.

When it is finally time for presents, I distribute mine first since they're the easiest. I have envelopes for all, a standard ADC envelope. Sounds boring, but each one has a very cute gift sticker courtesy of Citibank, who thoughtfully provided a sheet of them in the December issues of several magazines I receive. Two sheets came through unscathed before the mailroom discovered unauthorized stickers and carefully peeled them off all of the sheets that arrived in the next magazines. God bless the mailroom officer.

What a sad way to make a living.

Each envelope has little treasures: a home-made Christmas card, a *Cartier* bookmark, and a plethora of perfume strips. What's a *Cartier* bookmark? About three weeks earlier, I received a Cartier catalogue in the mail filled with stunning photographs of jewelry, but that wasn't the attraction. The cover was constructed of heavy silk faille, backed with glossy silver paper. It was gorgeous, an art project waiting to happen. I took it to Gale whose eyes lit up. She is Ms. Arts and Crafts personified and has access to a paper cutter. She cut up the cover into two inch wide bookmarks. She then lettered **BELIEVE** in beautiful calligraphy with a gold pen on the red silk side before handing them over to me. I designed the sentiment for the glossy side:

> ***Believe in God and believe in yourself.***
> ***Together you can do great things with love.***
> ***I believe in you.***

Those are precious words for anyone in prison. We often feel that nobody believes in us.

My gift to Meg is, of course, bigger. I created a journal for her with a bright yellow brief cover and a pad of paper I managed to get three-hole punched. I made a special cover sheet with yellow construction paper and wrote inspirational quotes on the top of the first twenty pages. I also tucked in a bookmark and some perfume strips. Those are particularly prized because we are definitely sensory-deprived. (About three months earlier, the mailroom decided perfume strips were contraband and began tearing them out of all the magazines. Nothing like a little busy work for a short staff. As you can imagine, there was a huge protest. What harm is there in perfume strips? Finally, cooler heads prevailed and perfume strips were approved again, but no cute stickers. Those are definitely a threat to public safety.)

All of us receive treasures to open. Meg commissioned our neighbor to create Christmas cards individualized for each of us. Kristy's has a sketch of her beloved puppy. Kirsten's has a hot car surrounded by lots of shopping bags. Stacy's has a soccer ball, Chinese food, and cocktails by a swimming pool. My card includes all my favorite books, pets, a fireplace, and David flying a Stearman overhead. It is perfect. For each of us, the gifts are appropriate to our needs. Stamps and writing supplies for me. She knows me well.

As the moon rises over the razor wire, I am struck with how beautiful it looks; the bright, translucence contrasts with the stark grays and shadows of the prison yard. It is Christmas Eve in prisons all over the world and I pray for those inmates less fortunate, in Super Max, in dirty jails, in third world countries, freezing, dirty, hungry, alone. We are warm, we are fed, and we have each other. I count my blessings.

A group of carolers spontaneously starts to sing and I join them as they go from pod to pod, singing the old favorites. We aren't very good, but we are loud and enthusiastic, especially with Jingle Bells. Everyone knows that. It is the perfect ending to a joyful day. But there is more. When I return to my room, I find two secret Santa gifts for me. One is a darling little red and green basket filled with Hershey kisses. It is really a pop-tart box carefully covered with strips of red and green paper in a basket weave design with a woven handle. The other is a three dimensional stocking made from a manila folder, beautifully painted with a Christmas mouse who winks at me. The stocking alone is gift enough, but it is filled with treats including a little paper box holding the most delicious fudge. I am overwhelmed with love and thanksgiving. It is Christmas Eve in prison.

Christmas Day starts with brunch, but I am anticipating Bible study. Genny, our regular volunteer arranged her schedule to be with us this morning, bringing music, decorations, and communion. She chooses to come to prison on Christmas morning and we are all deeply grateful. I am grateful for the peace of my faith and for the dedication of volunteers like Genny who give of themselves so generously. We all feel the spirit of Christmas in the stark classroom as we pray.

The rest of the weekend involves watching *It's a Wonderful Life* for the umpteenth time, thankful like George Bailey to be alive. On Boxing Day, I have a lovely visit with my friend Carolyn, who chooses to make the long drive to prison over the holidays to see me. What a glorious Christmas gift. While the rest of the world compares shiny new toys and bling, at Perryville we are grateful for the homemade treasures and creativity we share. From nothing, we manage to make something, and the memories will last a lifetime. Away from the hustle and bustle, the competition, the message of *"gimmie,"* we understand the true spirit of Christmas, one to keep in our hearts always . . . *inside and out.*

Chapter 16

New Year's Eve

December 2004. For all our years together, David and I always celebrated New Year's Eve at home. No loud parties, no big crowds, no kissing strangers at midnight. We had a tradition. I always decorated with colorful New Year's paraphernalia, setting the table with our best and adding noisemakers and silly hats, crystal bowls full of streamers and confetti, and bright balloons tied to the backs of our chairs. We even followed tradition in what we wore. David wore his favorite black cashmere turtleneck sweater and I wore my favorite ancient black sequined skirt that thankfully had an elastic waistband. I loved that skirt; it aged with me.

While I decorated the table, David carefully planned the music: Frank Sinatra, Glen Miller, João Gilberto, Linda Ronstadt, and hits of the 60's. He then laid the logs in the fireplace while I prepped the salad, the vegetables, and the dessert. Then I took a nap because otherwise I would not have made it to midnight. About 8:30, we'd meet in the living room for cocktails and a dance. It was our night to focus completely on each other. We danced and talked through dinner. David always grilled steaks and we enjoyed our simple but delicious meal.

At eleven, we'd get out pens and paper. We each wrote down the bad things that happened the previous year and then our goals and dreams for the coming year. This is a Brazilian tradition, but theirs is more dramatic. Brazilians place their lists in very small boats. Imagine a boat for Barbie. They decorate them with flowers and candy or tiny gifts. Then, dressed in white, they go down to the beaches like Copacabana and Ipanema and at midnight launch their boats into the ocean as offerings to the goddess of the sea. If your boat sails out successfully, the goddess accepts your offering and it will be a good year. If, however, your boat comes crashing in on a wave, the goddess isn't pleased and your future won't be so great.

Imagine, midnight in Rio, everyone dressed in flowing white, enjoying the warm summer breeze, carrying their boats, humble or lavish, filled with colorful flowers and candy. It just seemed joyful to me. David and I never made it to Rio for New Year's, but I decided we'd take the best of it and make it another part of our tradition. We wrote our lists and made a tiny boat out of a milk carton, decorating it with bougainvillea from the garden and little votive candles. We lived right by the canal and at midnight, we'd walk over and launch our little boat, watching it bob merrily down the dark water. I assured David that eventually our fragile boat would make it to the sea.

Now I am at Perryville, surrounded by concrete and gravel, miles from water, wondering how in the world to celebrate New Year's Eve. I decide to invite my four young friends to meet at the picnic table at 6:30 and bring pen and paper. Stacy thoughtfully makes hot cocoa for us. It is very cold, but they are curious. "Close your eyes and imagine we're in Rio de Janeiro." I tell them. "It's summer. It's New Year's Eve. We're all dressed in white, happy to be together."

As I describe the events of a Brazilian New Year's, I can see by their smiles that I have captured their imaginations. I encourage them to think about 2004 and write down the bad stuff that we want to get rid of. Everyone agrees it is a short list, prison and separation from loved ones. Next we write our goals and dreams for 2005. Each of the four ladies will be released within the next six months so this is actually an important exercise. Writing goals will help them visualize and focus. I tell them to think carefully about how they see their lives. What is important to them now? All is quiet as they labor over their papers in the very dim light of the yard.

As I watch them, I am pleased and a little relieved. I was afraid they might think this was corny, but, on the contrary, they embrace it seriously. It is a good time to set their goals. I'm pleased that they want to share. We go around the table, listening and encouraging each other. And when we are done, we join hands as I pray over our little group of friends and our precious dreams; that God will look favorably on them when they leave prison and will bless them on their journey.

It is late and we are frozen, but no one wants to leave. It is a significant moment in our time here, to always treasure.

"But what about our papers and the ocean, Sue Ellen? What are we going to do?"

In prison we have to be creative. When we go inside for count, I figure we will just have to tear up our papers and sprinkle the little bits into the toilet. It is water and surely one flush will eventually make it to the sea. Laughingly, we agree this is a great idea. Yes, it is prison, it is ugly, it is cold and awful, but imagination is a wonderful thing . . . *inside and out.*

Chapter 17

The Rabbit Hole

January 2005. Sometimes in prison I feel like I am Alice and I have fallen down the Rabbit Hole into Wonderland. There is a brown queen yelling, "Off with her head. Send her to the hole." There are all manner of brown palace guards to protect the queen and do her bidding. And the mad tea party goes on endlessly. So often, there are no rational explanations for things, so it must be Prison Wonderland.

One day a C.O. tells Donna that she has to turn in her appliances. Donna is shocked. Turning in appliances means loss of privileges and this is connected to a ticket. She has no ticket. She knows it's a mistake. Also, it is Super Bowl weekend and Donna is a huge sports fan. She tells the C.O. it's a mistake.

"Too bad," he says. "You still have to turn in your appliances and you can get it straightened out on Monday."

Donna wants to speak to a sergeant, our right in case of a dispute. Very displeased, the C.O. radios his sergeant that the inmate is refusing to turn in her appliances and demanding to speak to him. "Okay, send her up," the sergeant says.

At the yard office, the sergeant checks the computer and sure enough, Donna is ticket-free. It is a mistake. She doesn't have to turn in her appliances, but the sergeant issues her a ticket for refusing to obey a direct order to turn in her appliances — that she didn't have to turn in the first place. Yes, it was a mistake, but since she refused to obey the mistake, she gets a ticket and loses her TV after all. Staff is paranoid about direct orders. If a C.O. gives you a direct order, no matter how outrageous it may be, if we disobey it, we get a ticket. In a rational world, the sergeant would have acknowledged the mistake and sent Donna on her way, maybe even apologized. That's out of the question in prison.

Now here's the clincher. When Donna goes to the disciplinary hearing, she gets a little lecture and the ticket is dismissed. It was a lot of paperwork for nothing, but that's how things work in Prison Wonderland.

Inmates are not allowed to carry anything in their pockets to work except tobacco and toilet paper. Say you're trying to quit smoking and want to carry some hard candy. Nope. Cigarettes are okay; hard candy is not. Chap Stick? Forget about it. A pen to use at work? Nope, they should be furnished (but they aren't). What about diabetics and hypo-glycemics? Can they carry candy? Nope. Well, maybe. No one seems to agree on that one. I'm hypoglycemic, so I carry hard candy and hope for the best. I am pushing the envelope because I also carry Chap Stick and a pen. These items are a big threat to public safety, at least in Prison Wonderland.

Soup cups are another Prison Wonderland game. The store sells this Ramen-like soup in Styrofoam cups. We re-use the cups in all manner of ways. We put our cheap plastic official cup in it so the Styrofoam one becomes an insulator. It keeps the official cup from sweating all over our *fine steel furniture*. We use it to boil water with our stinger so we won't burn our hands when we pick up the hot cup. It's also an extra serving bowl in a pinch. They're very handy. But at every shake, the empty Styrofoam cups are gleefully tossed. They seem to be a red flag. One C.O. told me they were a good hiding place. Good grief, these girls are more ingenious than that. As long as they sell the soup, inmates will be using those cups. During the shakes, they toss them out in the morning, and by noon everyone has a new one. It's a Prison Wonderland game.

Bartering and trading, which is against ADC policy, is another Wonderland game. It's another red flag. When I arrived, I was indigent; no money, no job, no nothing. But the C.O. at State Issue (where we are given our prison wardrobe) said I must turn in the shower shoes I was issued at R & A and buy the 65¢ ones from the prison store. How am I supposed to do that without job or money? I think with horror that I will have to go barefooted, a guarantee for athlete's foot in the grimy showers.

One of the inmate clerks who works at State Issue offers to buy the shower shoes for me, right in front of the officer! We've been warned that this is considered bartering and trading. Even worse, she wants me to be in her debt. I am painfully green as grass. I look around for help. The officer nods her head in agreement.

"Come back next week", she says, "and be ready to exchange shoes." Her tone is commanding.

I do as I am told. I return and exchange shoes, all with the unofficial blessing of one of the strictest C.O.s on the yard. Welcome to Prison Wonderland. They bend the rules to suit.

The bartering and trading rule is ridiculous, particularly on a female unit. Women don't barter, they give and giving is forbidden. I was penniless for several months when I first arrived and I'll never forget the generosity of these women I didn't even know. I was deathly ill from chemo and my lips were cracked and bleeding. I received gifts of Chap Stick, crackers, soup, and ginger-ale from the generosity of their hearts, with no expectations. They were gifts. But, if a C.O. had been in a bad mood, we could all have been ticketed.

Believe it or not, I got a ticket once. I call it the famous *Reader's Digest* ticket. My friend Carolyn gave me a highly prized subscription to *Reader's Digest,* and at Christmas, they sent me an incredible offer. I could send five subscriptions to people I knew for ten dollars. I was ecstatic. I submitted the names of two women I was tutoring in reading, knowing they could use the stimulation and inspiration of Reader's Digest to help them in their lessons.

I sent the form to Carolyn who added three more names, including my husband's, and the ten dollars to *Reader's Digest.* In January, during mail call, I was advised of a ticket. It seems the magazine had arrived and on the mailing label, it said *A gift from Sue Ellen Allen to Mary Jones.* Obviously, we were bartering and trading. And poor Mary, who knew nothing of my gesture, got a ticket too. As I've said before, reading is discouraged in prison.

When I called Carolyn, she was indignant. She called the ADW. It was, after all, her money and her subscription. *Yes, she had the cancelled check to prove it.* Mary and I had to sit in the disciplinary line and listen to a lecture on what rotten, scheming, miserable human beings we were to break this rule, but the tickets were dropped. Meanwhile, Joanne Smith, the other recipient on my list, got her magazine just fine without comment or ticket. Of course she did, it's Prison Wonderland!

Prison Wonderland is full of convoluted rules. Often, they only succeed in causing confusion, bad morale, and a lot of unnecessary paperwork. There is no doubt that there are some bad women in prison who look for trouble and seem to delight in breaking the rules, but the majority are confused, frightened, and just want to do the best they can to get out of here with their sanity intact. There are a lot of rules and punishments for the first group, but absolutely no rewards for the latter. There are no honor dorms, no trustee jobs, no increases in privileges if you're good. It's one size fits all and the result is a sort of negative apathy. Why try? Why bother? Inmates think, *Nothing I do matters in Prison Wonderland.*

In that regard, I keep swimming upstream believing, hoping that it does matter. People tell me I can't fight the system, but I keep trying and little by little, step-by-step, I win small battles. When I ask if we can have a *Santa Cruz Walk for the Cure* to raise money for breast cancer, everyone (myself included) is shocked when it is approved. ADW Bailey took a big risk by approving it. The walk has since spread to all the Arizona prisons and has raised over $100,000 for the American Cancer Society.

When I entered Perryville with cancer, I was desperate for a support group. Although there were fifteen of us suffering with advanced stages of cancer, pitifully eager for support and compassion, everyone said a support group would never happen. For one year, I worked on getting approval, mostly by begging and generally humiliating myself. Finally the *Santa Cruz Cancer Support Group* was approved and I'm told that the American Cancer Society (ACS) still sponsors it. When I was there, they were wonderful to us. They told me that ours was the only group of its kind in prison, sponsored by the ACS.

I had another vision that finally succeeded after a year of proposals and pleading. Outside, I was a member of both *Toastmasters International* and the *National Speakers Association.* I know what confidence one can build in learning speaking skills. *Toastmasters* has a provision for institutions called *Gavel Clubs* and I wanted to start one at Perryville. I knew it would provide great motivation and inspiration to those women willing to join. For another year, I wrote more kites to the authorities, again going through the begging and humiliation process. I refused to give up and one year later, I had the approval. That group is still going strong, has touched many lives, and has spread to other yards.

Finally, I pushed the envelope to the limit. I asked if we could have a *Life Skills* course. I was now an old number and had proven myself, so the approval came quickly. With my very good friends, Valerie and Tracey, we designed a curriculum for a fourteen week course that encompassed many subjects we thought the women here should know to help them upon release. We included Creative Writing, Art Appreciation, Personal and Business Etiquette, Jobs, Civics, Community Involvement, and Values. *The Life Skills* course has touched many lives over the years and is still being taught by inmates at Santa Cruz.

One person can make a difference, even in prison, even against razor wire odds that many say are insurmountable. Truly, sometimes they are, but not always. Sometimes, when you have a vision, you just have to stay focused against the odds, swim upstream, and ignore the nay-sayers.

I don't know why people want to rain on other people's parades, tearing down ideas and destroying dreams. Think how difficult it is to compose a symphony, write a book, or paint a picture, and how easy it is to criticize it. Critics are a dime a dozen, especially in Prison Wonderland, but we don't have to join them. We can be builders, doers, and dreamers anywhere. We can make a difference because what we do does matter . . . *inside or out.*

Chapter 18

Despair

March 2005. Despite my activities and optimistic spirit, I was lonely after Gina died and when I longed for a kindred spirit, God sent Laura, just four doors down. Highly educated with degrees in philosophy and political science, Laura had been married to a lobbyist in Washington, D.C. and had worked as a congressional aide. Daily we get our exercise by walking monotonous circles on the yard, but our stimulating conversations make the time zip by. I wished for intelligent conversation and Laura arrived practically on my doorstep, but truly I wouldn't have wished prison on anyone.

Laura is cursed with rheumatoid arthritis and fibromyalgia. She lives with constant pain and stiffness which she tries to combat with yoga and walking. Years ago, she became addicted to prescription painkillers, like Rush Limbaugh and so many women I've seen on Oprah and Dr. Phil. Eventually she started calling in fake prescriptions to the pharmacy and ended up in Perryville. Rush went to rehab, and Oprah and Dr. Phil give away free counseling and free trips to rehab for a fortunate few, but too many like Laura end up in prison. Not a very good use of taxpayer's money.

When Laura was in our hideous county jail, she plunged into the depths of depression, knowing she had humiliated herself and her family who, in their own combination of pain, pride, and snobbery, let her know she was a selfish monster. They basically abandoned her. Exhausted, alone, and in unbearable physical and emotional pain, Laura decided she did not deserve to live. In desperation, in her small isolation cell on the filthy mattress, she broke her glasses, slashed her wrists with the glass, and curled up to die. When a guard discovered her later covered with blood, he kicked her and snarled, "You bitch! Look at the mess you've made." She was promptly dragged up, treated with some steri-strips, and taken to the Psych ward of the jail. There she was four-pointed for the weekend which, with her Medical condition, was akin to torture.

Four-pointing is something you might expect to hear about in Abu Ghraib, but surely not here. They lay you on your back on an army cot with your arms and legs spread eagle and your wrists and ankles contained in ancient leather cuffs once lined in sheep skin that has long since disintegrated. You are spoon fed and only allowed up to go to the bathroom every four or five hours. Of course, after lying so long like that, your limbs stiffen horribly and you must be held up on both sides to attempt to walk. The pain is unbearable. The jail treats all its suicides this way. Finally, when you are practically comatose from the pain, they strip you and put you in a freezing cold isolation cell with just a plastic mattress and a small padded blanket like moving companies use. No heat. No clothes. No sheets. No compassion.

The so-called treatment is more like scare tactics. "By God, we'll terrify you into behaving." Who cares if you are bi-polar or psychotic? You get the same barbaric treatment. One of my friends is a volunteer at the jail Psych ward where she cuts hair about once a month. She says the screams and moans of those four-pointed inmates are heart-breaking. No one talks to them while they are four-pointed, there is no counseling, nor are they allowed to talk to a priest or pastor.

Suddenly Laura is on my yard, still depressed, still desperate and, as she says, given to very dark moods. She was diagnosed years ago as severely bi-polar, but at Perryville she receives neither medication nor counseling. Over the years, she's been on many meds and knows what works and what doesn't. An outside physician wrote to the Medical Department on her behalf about her reactions to various drugs, but Medical will not accept his observations. ADC's formulary drug is lithium and she can take that or nothing. Laura knows that lithium will speed up her system and cause hyper-reactions. The adverse reactions frighten her so she refuses it. "Ok, too bad. You get zip." So she shakes all the time. She tries to counteract the depression and darkness by walking and reading, reading and walking. She feels helpless and afraid.

One day when I go to walk with her, she asks to be alone.

"I'm not very good company today," she says.

Later, I drop by her room with a little homemade card and some magazines and she starts to cry. I insist that she come out to talk. For a long while, she talks and I listen. She has just learned that ADC has lost her son's application to visit, sent in six weeks ago. She is devastated. Her son is the only family member who hasn't abandoned her and she is desperate to talk to him. She can't call him until he is approved and the papers are lost. It normally takes eight weeks for visitor approval and she is due for release in eight weeks so to send another application is pointless. She is a mother separated from her eighteen-year-old son because of ADC's draconian policies and she is despondent. She doesn't want to live in this world.

This isn't the first barrier she's come up against recently. ADC barriers are a dime a dozen and Laura is convinced that she is being punished for her mistakes; that either there is no God or God hates her for her sins. She is exhausted, sobbing, broken by the system. I listen, broken by her pain. Finally she runs out of words and it is my turn, but what can I say?

God, please guide my words, I pray, as I acknowledge her very raw pain. She has been abandoned by her family and the system. She is entitled to her grief, but she is wrong about God. I tell her stories of others in here who suffer and grieve. I remind her how special she is, how wonderfully bright. She has so much to offer. Maybe her family is gone for now, but nothing is forever. I tell her about my grandfather who, in severe pain coupled with depression, committed suicide. I was just a baby, but my mother told me years later how traumatic it was for her. She found his body, blown apart by a shotgun, and had to deal with it all. Mother inherited some of my grandfather's depression. She always saw the glass as half empty. She fought depression all her life and told me she had often considered suicide, but said the memory of my grandfather's actions stopped her. She didn't want to put me or my father through that trauma.

Laura listens. She is thinking of her son and the rest of her family too. She hears my point. She does not want to level that kind of hurt upon them.

And what about God? Has God abandoned her? Is she being punished? I don't believe that. I don't believe all this mindless cruelty is from God, but I do believe we have the power to use it for

God. Her experiences can surely be used to comfort another who is desperate just as my experiences during my mastectomy, chemo, and radiation now help others facing it. It's like the old T-shirt — **Been there, done that**. The tag line should read, **Now how can I help?**

That's what this is all about. **Now how can I help?** When we've been there, when we've done all that, when we've walked through the mine fields and suffered a few explosions, then it is our opportunity to guide and comfort those fellow travelers who find themselves paralyzed with fear in the middle of that same mine field. Turn the pain into power though helping someone else.

I'm not qualified to try and explain life's suffering, but I can encourage loving thy neighbor as the answer to the suffering. The first line of F. Scott Peck's book *The Road Less Traveled* says, "Life is difficult." But comfort and compassion can make it less so. The late Pope John Paul II called for a "civilization of love." The Dalai Lama says, "My only religion is kindness." This isn't just religious lip service; it is surely the only way to survive. When the guards and the guarded, the victim and the offender, the friend and the foe see that we are all interconnected, see through the eyes of compassion, with that awesome insight and power, the world will shift . . . *inside and out.*

Chapter 19

Television

April 2005. This is the week my world changed in an amazing and unexpected way. After nearly three years of living in a bubble, I have a television! And not just any TV; I have a colored television. Suddenly in our tiny shoebox, there is a 13″ moving picture of color. The blues are so bright; the reds are so vivid; the pinks take my breath away. I am mesmerized by the M&M commercial. I had no idea I was so sensory deprived, but our world is drab . . . all gray and brown and cream splashed with the violent, yet, oh-so-fashionable orange ensemble that we wear for security.

It happens to be the week of Pope John Paul II's funeral and I am riveted to CNN. The pageantry and history are compelling, and the colors of the Pope's robe and the Cardinal's hats and cassocks are glorious. Following that, I intend to catch Charles and Camilla's wedding just so I can delight in those fantastic hats that British ladies are prone to wear to weddings.

This little TV has changed the quality of my sentence. It brings the news to me in a timely manner instead of what I read in *TIME* magazine a week later. Thoreau said he felt it was pointless to read a newspaper more than once in his life because the news was always the same, but I don't live at Walden Pond. I want to feel a part of the world, even in prison.

The TV also brings laughter into my life again. The serious and fearful prison environment has permeated my spirit and I have become ultra-serious, rarely laughing. Suddenly I am watching *Oprah* and *Ellen* and the world is brighter. Reruns of *Friends* and *M*A*S*H* cause me to laugh out loud. It feels great. It is also sheer luxury to see the colors — in the clothes, the food and the scenery. Of course, seeing a food commercial for something delicious that includes fruits and vegetables causes a deep longing within. But never mind, I know I'll eat a tomato again someday.

I delight in this new accessory in our shoebox. How did I get it on my lavish salary of 30¢ an hour? I did something really tacky. I thought about it for a long time and finally decided, *Oh, heck, what could be tackier than prison?* and I asked for help. I have several friends who write to me, always asking what they can send me to make my life better. Truthfully, there isn't much anyone can do. We're only allowed to receive money orders or magazine subscriptions, books or tapes from a proper store, so I always just say *Thanks, I'm fine.* Finally, I gather my courage and write to each of them that if they all pool their resources, I can get a TV.

It was the tsunami that hit on December 26, 2004, that pushed me. During that nightmare of a crisis, I longed to see the news. I realized I was tired of living in a bubble so I asked, and when I dropped the letters in the mail box, I said a little prayer that no one would think I was outrageously cheeky for asking. To my utter delight, within ten days, everyone had generously contributed and I was happily walking back to the yard lugging the official ADC model TV. It's a clear plastic box with a 13″ screen, designed so nothing can be hidden from prying eyes.

It is nothing anyone in the outside world would buy at any price, but in prison ADC sells it for the princely sum of $199.80, an outrageous price for inmates who make such meager salaries. Nevertheless, you cannot imagine how much pleasure I get from that small plastic box. It is my connection to the outside world and I feel very blessed.

Does that mean I am now a couch potato, vegging in front of every soap opera and game show? No, I am still among the world's most voracious readers and the library's best customer. I enjoy wonderful magazine subscriptions too, thanks to my lovely friends. I am too busy during the day to turn the TV on, but when the proper time comes, CNN and PBS are my channels of choice. I wish there was one channel that just showed gorgeous scenery and played classical music, or maybe just Andre Boccelli and Sinatra. Then I might be tempted to have it on all the time.

In the real world, many people have huge flat screen TVs in nearly every room. It's always on; it entertains, it educates, it influences us in a million subtle ways, but it's taken for granted. I doubt, however, if I will ever take it for granted again. While I do lament the inaneness of too many shows, the violence and the stupidity, I also applaud its power to bring the world to us, to make us part of the global community. Even in prison, isolated and cut off, thanks to that little TV, I am a part of the world again. I am seeing history, I am learning, I am laughing, I am grateful for the generosity of friends who brought the world to me.

They say when you go to prison you learn who your friends really are and I would certainly agree. It's awesome and humbling to experience that type of friendship. As much as I love words, there are none sufficient enough, emotionally strong enough, to express my feelings about these friends who reach out to me behind the walls, to acknowledge me as a human being. I urge you to honor your friends and treat them with respect and love, for friendship is a precious thing . . . *inside and out.*

Chapter 20

Mega-Shake

April 2005. The buzz spread across the yard like a swarm of bees, loud and fierce. A major shake is coming, a nightmare shake to end all shakes. Why? We just had our quarterly shake a month ago. This, however, is a statewide shake ordered by the Director after serious contraband was found at Florence Prison. What was found remains a mystery, but rumor has it that weapons, a cell-phone, and a laptop were found. A laptop! Heavens, I'd dance naked for a typewriter. Okay, that's a gross exaggeration, but I would be very excited. Whatever they found sparked enough interest to schedule this mega-shake and our day is fast approaching.

At Perryville, rumor is king, or should I say queen? The rumors come at machine gun speed. The *Men in Black* are coming. They are like a SWAT team. They'll be yelling and screaming and using intimidation tactics to scare us. They'll destroy the rooms. They'll turn our storage boxes upside down and dump everything on the floor. The dogs are going to walk all over our beds. They are going to rip open our food items. I am horrified.

Let me explain the emotions of a shake. Inmates are among the most creative pack rats on the planet. Because we aren't allowed much, more is definitely better in an inmate's world. What we own would embarrass a homeless person — an extra white plastic spork (a weird, non-dangerous combination of spoon and fork for the inmate population), a Styrofoam soup cup, the extra bowl and cup we manage to hide for *cooking* tasks, an extra plastic pill bag for candy, an empty peanut butter jar to keep candy away from the bugs. It's all junk, but it's our junk and it helps keep our world tidy. It is also contraband. A peanut butter jar is only allowed when it has peanut butter in it. Once it's empty, using it for candy is forbidden. Same with the soup cup; in prison, recycling is not allowed.

Then there is the problem of extra books and magazines. I constantly chaff at the severe restriction of five magazines and seven books. It is actually my only sin in prison. I always have too many. It never ceases to amaze me that a place exists in the United States of America where books are seriously restricted. Extra books are contraband and I have to find places for them. I farm mine out to the girls who don't read. They are happy to keep my cherished books and once the shake is over, back they come. My contraband is pretty simple. The old numbers have more serious stuff that they have stashed God knows where; tweezers, needles, cigarette lighters; all forbidden, all treasured, and all here.

In Arizona, all prisons have a quarterly shake. Inmates are locked down for the day as yard by yard, room by room, we are searched. It's supposed to be a surprise, but it never is. The word comes down through the inmate grapevine and Spring Cleaning commences. Prized contraband is tossed or hidden and by the time Shake Day arrives, we are ready.

Prepped or not, inmates hate shakes. It's disruptive and invasive, but that's prison. So when we hear the announcement for C pod to get ready, we dutifully march out to the fence and line up while the dogs sniff us and the officers ransack our cells. Then it's over for three months and we get more soup cups and sporks, we retrieve our books, and things go back to normal.

Until now, the mega-shake. They are going to look for hidden weapons in all the nooks and crannies. This is a set-up waiting to happen. If someone doesn't like you (inmates or staff), they can sneak in your room and hide something really outrageous like a needle or a shank. To be safe, we look under the bunks and behind the drawers and shelves just in case there's something hidden from years ago. I reorganize my storage boxes and farm out my books. I am ready

Shake Day dawns. The bus of extra C.O.'s arrives very early and they start at the other end of the yard. That means we will be last. My heart pounds until I realize I am being ridiculous. God said, "Fear Not" and there is no reason to be afraid. It's just stuff and pretty pitiful stuff at that. I survived Estrella, and the dungeon, and a mastectomy under nightmarish conditions. God has always been with me and I know I can do this. I pray over the room and settle down for the long wait.

We are locked down for thirty-six hours, during which time we get ADC room service; what the girls euphemistically call "bag-nasties" (yucky sandwiches, a bag of stale chips, and a dry cookie). Many women go slightly stir-crazy. I am perfectly content reading, writing, and watching my magical new television. My roommate Elizabeth sleeps. She is without a doubt the best sleeper I have ever seen. She can sleep for days through noise and light. If there was an Olympic category for sleeping, Elizabeth would win the Gold. I am envious.

Finally, at 9:45 the next day, we hear the bullhorn for C pod. I am ready. I have stripped my bed, emptied my drawer and folded everything neatly on top of the desk. At the front of my few possessions I have placed the special box in which I keep my prescription bras for my prosthesis. On top of the box is my own personal brown rubber breast. When the officers see that, it makes them uncomfortable and they generally leave us alone.

The doors pop open and we are called out very professionally. Surprise. There is no yelling and the officers are in regular brown; no black in sight. We are almost politely escorted to a corner room to be strip searched. The officers are quick and efficient; soon we are dressed and in another line against the fence, waiting for the dogs.

Sniff, sniff, done. We then wait while some officers search the rooms and others rake the pebbles on the yard looking for hidden treasures. While we are waiting, I notice a sudden congregation right outside our room in front of the small closet that houses the plumbing between the rooms. The DW and ADW and finally, even the Warden of Perryville are all there. It wasn't until later that we learn they found two shanks in the closet. I am told they looked very old and the Powers decided they must have been left over from the days when men were housed here. Shanks are more a male thing. Women aren't so violent; they would rather gossip and tattle.

Soon the excitement is over and we are locked back in our rooms. Elizabeth and I are speechless with joy. Our room has hardly been touched and nothing was thrown away, not our extra bowl or cups or empty peanut butter jar. Our pitiful treasures are all here. It doesn't take long before our beds are remade, our drawers arranged, and we're back to normal. We are hugely relieved. All those rumors of terror were just that, fuel to feed the fires of boredom. By dinner time, it is all over and we are free from the confines of the room. I come away a little wiser. I must stay away from the rumor mill and the inmate hysteria, no matter how seductive. Ignoring gossip is always a good idea . . . *inside and out.*

Chapter 21

Moving On

July 2005. My roommate, Candace, is leaving tomorrow. Red Letter Day. She is going home. There's been a countdown of months, weeks, days, and now, hours. The last week of horrid food, last day of work, last classes, and last finals. A lot of lasts. Then, when she walks through those gates for the last time, she'll be faced with a barrage of firsts. She's lost everything and will start from Ground Zero with zero.

She receives a $50 check as she leaves. It's not tax-payer's money. This money was garnished from her 30¢ per hour job. As soon as she leaves, she has to pay her parole officer $103 in monthly supervision fees. She's in the hole before she starts. And she has a two-year old son and she needs a job, a place to live, transportation, and even clothes. You see, the debt to society does not end with your time served. It continues its very long reach into your life. She will always be an ex-felon. The city is full of crime-free areas where she can never live despite how good she is. Many companies won't hire an ex-con. Most licenses cannot be regained even if the crime is unrelated. (In Arizona, she cannot be a barber, nail technician, or mortician, just a few on a very long list.) So where can she go and what can she do?

All of us on the inside feel her anxiety. We all want to be free, but it's a rare inmate who has a life to return to outside. Most lives and families have been destroyed. Most have nothing. We are anxious for her because we are anxious for ourselves. How will she make it? Is there hope for us?

Meanwhile, life inside goes on. Candace has been a terrific roommate, completely stress-free and low-maintenance, a real blessing. My first two years at Perryville I had a revolving door of roommates, many of them seriously lacking in communication skills. Those times were very lonely. No one to talk to about life and love, books and art, politics and travel and all the other ands.

Some of my roommates were good; some not so good. People have asked me if race was involved in my roommate relationships. Race was never an issue. I've had white, black, and brown roommates and what made them good or bad was not their skin color, but their character (with all due respect to Martin Luther King, Jr.). Underneath skin tone is a human being with all the joys and sorrows of everyone else. Color has nothing to do with kindness, consideration, respect, sense of humor, attitude, and love.

In prison, you watch out for the-not-so-good ones who demonstrate what the prison calls *issues*. Mostly, it's anger issues. That can get scary. Roommates can make life in prison agreeable or disastrous. Honestly, I had so many; I've forgotten some of their names. It was confusing, during a time when I yearned for stability.

In that revolving door, Gina was not my first roommate, but she was my first blessing. I was thirty-two years her senior and wondered what we could possibly share? A lot, as it turned out. We loved to write. We loved to laugh. We were both on a spiritual path and became prayer partners. Every night we sat facing each other and held hands as we talked to God. We talked like God was sitting in that tiny room with us. Our conversation was sometimes puzzled, sometimes pissed off, but always grateful for life. When we finished, Gina would give me a big hug and say, "That was beautiful, Sue Ellen." She was such a lovely soul who I know is now spreading her joy in heaven. I still miss her.

Melissa became my next care-giver. Melissa and I had been roommates at Estrella Jail. She was pregnant there and suffering from serious depression. She had her baby under the sheriff's care. Shackled during her delivery, she was not allowed to touch her new daughter when she was born. The hospital allows it, but the sheriff does not. I cannot imagine the pain of that immediate and wrenching separation.

When Gina died, I was right in the middle of radiation and my chest was a mass of blisters and raw, peeling skin. Melissa immediately offered to move in and become my care-giver. Many times a day, she would painstakingly coat my burns with a special burn cream. It was a brutally hot summer with many days over 115 degrees in a stifling room without even a fan. She made cool compresses for me and, feeling helpless, tried to ease my excruciating pain as best she could, both of us sweating and miserable. During a very hard time, she was my second blessing.

As the revolving door whirled around, Candace became my third blessing. She knew how to laugh at the absurdity of this place. She loved to entertain her little group of friends, seeking any resource to present things beautifully. Well, beautiful is definitely too strong a word, but she made things festive and pretty and her wide smile brightened everything.

So who will be next? Department of Corrections doesn't do courtesy moves. That is, they refuse to put two congenial friends together. We're supposed to take potluck. But potluck often results in disaster and extra moves when two women come to blows.

My first roommate was a very beautiful, petite, blue eyed blond. She looked like a Botticelli angel when she smiled, which was rare. Although only twenty-eight years old, she was a very old number, tough as nails. She had no patience for me, a very new number. She saw fit to embellish my crime and told everyone I had been a cat burglar in Europe and was on America's Most Wanted List. Of course, this made me a really old cat burglar, but the truth is irrelevant in prison.

Before I'd even opened my mouth, she'd decided she loathed me and simply refused to speak to me. I couldn't imagine what I'd done. I'd only just arrived and she scared the hell out of me. I sat curled in the corner of my bunk feeling pathetic. The air in the tiny room was thick with her hostility and I was miserable. When I went to the counselor for help, I was told to suck it up and learn to get along. Remember, No Courtesy Moves. A few days later, I was moved. Delighted, but puzzled, I happily took my meager belongings three doors down. The old number had what I learned was a *big juice card*, which means in prison, a lot of influence.

In rapid succession, the roommate-revolving-door whirled. I had a cheerful young woman who was immediately reclassified and moved to another yard, followed by the young bank robber with the anger issues. I never knew when her next eruption would occur and my already frayed nerves, frayed further still. The Teflon Kid miraculously avoided disciplinary action for a time, but finally even the officers had enough. She was hauled off for six months in CDU and peace reigned as Gina moved in.

And then Gina was gone and the door whirled faster. Candace

followed Melissa and so many others during my seven years. They all touched my life and I will never forget them. Each one brought her own story with her, filling the room with emotions so deep and often so painful that I couldn't imagine their struggles. Living in a tiny room under very difficult conditions, they taught me a lot. Love and compassion and lots of patience, lessons I am grateful to have . . . *inside and out.*

Chapter 22

Roommate Square Dance

July 2005. Early Monday morning, Candace leaves. We hug and she is gone without a backward glance. The room feels empty. We don't have much, but what we do have makes the room (sort of) cozy. Pictures on the bulletin board, sodas and chips from the store, books, shampoo, and a clock all contribute to the person who is Candace. I fuss around, straightening, cleaning, and waiting for the next occupant. As soon as one leaves, there are dozens more in the tents outside sweating and hoping for a bed inside. Finally, I become impatient and go to the control booth to ask who's coming. "No one," I'm told. I have a single suite for the night. That is unheard of and everyone is envious. Even if you love your roommate, that kind of solitude is a luxury.

I am very anxious about who's next. A month ago, Meg and I put in a request to live together. I know I said no courtesy moves but I was hopeful. However, Meg should have been moved immediately, so I figure we are out of luck.

I spend a peaceful night, but it seems empty without Candace's cheerful chatter. On Tuesday morning about 10:30, the door tentatively slides open and I see a very tall young woman peek her head around. Before I can say, "Welcome," she says, "This won't do. I can't have a top bunk. I'm nine months pregnant." So off we go to the control booth to sort it out. Then back to await the decision of the higher-ups. Maybe this mistake will bring Meg.

Twenty minutes later, another face peers around the door. This time it's a very short, round woman in her 50's with a radiant smile. Mary bounds into the room with energy and enthusiasm and we instantly hit it off like old friends. She's just been released from R & A and, like me, has been praying for someone nice. Fortunately, she thinks I am it.

I am suddenly the old number in the room, so I show Mary the ropes and introduce her to the kitchen officers who do the hiring. She wants to work in the kitchen and my introductions lead to a job. She is very thankful for the help. Even in prison, it's really all about networking and who you know. Helping Mary reminds me how wonderful it is to serve.

Meanwhile, Meg is unhappy. She is desperate to get away from Janice, her roommate, who is a really Old Number. Most of our numbers are six digits; Janice's number is only five. She's been at Perryville a very long time and operates by a different code of conduct. She is grumpy and very abrupt in her dealings with the rest of us who she considers underlings. No patience, no people skills.

Meg is scared of her and spends a lot of time hiding out in our pod, afraid that Janice is going to find her to clean the room again. Janice is obsessive/compulsive, and the room is never clean enough. She makes Meg scrub the walls and even the ceilings and if she finds one stray hair, she throws a fit. More often than not, she also throws their only chair. Fortunately, it is indestructible plastic that can survive the abuse because she throws it a lot. Meg's hair is short but, after all, hair is hair and it sheds.

Why doesn't Janice clean? They both work, but Meg goes to school too, so Janice has more free time. Janice is a bully and she bullies Meg into doing everything for her. No one else would put up with that and her room has been a revolving door of roommates. Poor Meg, she cleans and then she hides. It is a little like Cinderella and the wicked step-mother, except there is no Fairy Godmother and no Prince Charming.

Meg's nerves are shot. She approached me about moving in when Candace leaves and it seemed like a good solution for both of us. I did, however, suggest that Janice needed an opportunity to also ask for a roommate of her choice. Meg was afraid to tell her she wanted to move. She was afraid life would become even more unbearable and the chair would fly again.

All this became a mute point when Mary moved in. Mary is thrilled with our easy companionship and has no desire to move. I know that once she gets the job in the kitchen, she'll be moved to the yard where all the kitchen workers live, but, ever hopeful, she puts in a request to stay. Meg is looking sadder by the day.

I didn't expect anything to happen for at least a week or two, but on Friday morning at 7:30, Mary is told to pack up and move. I am surprised at their efficiency. She just got the job and they usually don't move that fast. I help her pack and reach for my shoes. On my way to find out who's next, I meet a most excited Meg, all smiles and enthusiasm. She is moving in. I too am delighted and relieved. It was a tumultuous week and I am ready for some tranquility.

Tranquility is not on the menu. Janice is furious. She's been betrayed and Meg is a little rat. Big rat, actually. In my naïveté, I ignore the signs and begin to help Meg get settled. Suddenly, there is a figure in orange at the door.

"Thanks for giving my homey a heads up," snarls Pat, Janice's livid friend. They are feeding their anger and Janice orders me over to talk to her. Now, I must confess, Janice scares me too. In the few dealings I've had with her, she's been rude and sharp tongued. She works in the library and even checking out a book with her is an ordeal. Because I always anticipate rudeness, I try to cover her up with kindness. It never works. She thinks I am a wimp and treats me like I am lower than ants. I love the library, but Janice is the scorpion in the honey.

Nevertheless, in a moment of insanity, I go out to brave the lioness in her den. I am prepared to tell a lie to protect Meg and to avoid hurting Janice's feelings. Neither Meg nor I want to tell Janice the truth: that she is a miserable, angry, negative human being that scares the fool out of us, and Meg wanted to move. It wouldn't change anything and would only succeed in making things worse. So I tell her how surprised I am at the move, hating the lie and hating my fear. She is still furious. I use a tactic that everyone uses in prison, a scapegoat that I hate. I remind her that *it is prison* and they can do anything they want. She glares and snaps at me to get out of her face. Willingly I comply. It's an ugly scene and I leave shaking.

Back at the room, I start to worry. Some of these old numbers can resort to violence. I've heard of accidents happening, people beaten up in the showers, contraband planted in rooms, and anonymous kites written. My imagination goes wild. Meg assures me the fire will only blaze for a day and then there will be a new drama. Janice and her friends are all talk.

The next day I am out at 6:30 in the morning for breakfast. I have to walk past Janice and her group, already up for the first cigarette of the day. As I go by, I hear mumbling, "What a worthless piece of shit" . . . and other phrases too colorful to repeat. I hold my head up, breathe deeply, and keep walking. Thankfully, when I return, they are gone.

Meg and I are unsettled by all of this nastiness. It's one of the big fears of prison life. I decide to stop by Lisa's room for advice. Another old number, somehow she has managed to maintain her dignity and civility. She tells me not to worry. Janice is indeed all talk and will not try to hurt us.

"Sue Ellen, don't you know how many there are here who have your back." I did not know and I am deeply touched.

It was an interesting week. I am pleased I was able to help Mary and I've made a new friend. I am happy to have Meg as a roommate, but I am still afraid of Janice. When things get really bad, some smart aleck is always around to remind me that God won't give me more than I can handle. I wish God didn't have so much faith in me, but I do know I will survive and serve and that's a good lesson . . . *inside or out.*

Chapter 23

Further Down the Rabbit Hole

August 2005. One of the biggest adjustments for me living behind the wires is the amazing variety of rules in each jail and prison. They're all different depending on the administration and the personality of its leaders. Some rules make perfect sense and are designed to protect everyone: staff and inmates alike. Others border on insanity and are designed to make inmates' lives as miserable as possible. They harken back to the old philosophy of warehousing prisoners and do little to encourage inmates to make decisions or learn how to be responsible. A professor told me there is actually logic in ADC's illogical pattern that helps to create an atmosphere of imbalance and confusion amongst the inmates.

One of the most important elements of stability behind bars is mail. It's the link to children, family, and friends. It's a symbol that someone values you as a human being and can go a long way toward influencing an inmate's future.

Inmates are not allowed to write to any inmates in any other prisons nationwide. For example, Melissa was my roommate for nearly a year and we grew quite close. As soon as she moved to another yard, our communication was cut off. No further contact is allowed. To write to other family members that are also incarcerated, you must prove that you're a spouse, sibling, or parent.

It's okay to live together for years, but no communicating afterwards. The theory is that we shouldn't have anything to do with felons or ex-felons, but with 1 in 100 people now behind bars, the field for friends becomes seriously limited. I've known women who weren't allowed to live at home because someone else in the family was an ex-felon. Instead of being allowed to parole to their home where their family and children live and rent is free, they're forced to go to a half-way house where they must pay rent and where all the other residents are, you guessed it, ex-felons.

They even have the power to split up husbands and wives who've been married for years prior to their felony. This blanket policy is destructive, expensive, and cruel to enforce. But enforce it they do, often harshly. I knew a young woman released on parole who had a date with an ex-felon. It was a date, not a robbery or a murder or a DUI — a date. And where did she meet him? At her community service, filled with ex-felons. She had not committed a new crime. This is what is known as a technical violation of a parole rule. Her parole was revoked and she was returned to prison for two years. Previously, this young woman had been a model inmate. No record of disciplinary problems or poor attitude. And upon release, she was not a troublemaker. So, let's charge the tax payer about $40,000 to punish her for a date.

Next on my list of draconian rules has to do with books. Earlier I mentioned inmates are only allowed to own seven books and five magazines. They say this extraordinarily restrictive policy is for security measures, but again I think the pros far outweighed the cons. I've yet to hear of anyone using a book for a weapon, although I know getting smarter is definitely a tool for a brighter future. This leaves me baffled. Education is not encouraged in Arizona. After all, in the late nineties, the Legislature ordered that inmates must pass eighth grade education. If they do, they can get ninety days knocked off their sentence. That is eighth grade, not twelfth, not GED — **eighth grade**. What good will that do anyone in finding a job? You can't even say, "Do you want fries with that?"

It costs an average of $20,000 annually to house an inmate in Arizona. That's tuition in a good university, yet we cut the state education budget and increase the budget for prisons. According to a 1997 report by the Center on Crime, Communities, and Culture at the Open Society Institute, *inmates with at least two years of college education have a mere 10 percent re-arrest rate.* In April 2001, Fortune magazine cited a study that explored three decades of prison college education; it found that *every dollar spent on education resulted in $1.71 in reduced crime costs.**

There is another idiotic rule related to books that leaves me shaking my head. Our rooms are supposed to be Spartan. No comfort or color allowed. We are allowed to keep our TV, clock, and fan on the shelf by our bed, and we each have a shelf for store snacks. Everything else goes in our only drawer, including clothes, coat, hat, hygiene, books, and program materials. The drawers are stuffed. Consequently, it is very hard to find and access things quickly. Even if there is space on the snack shelf, we are not allowed to keep our books there. Consider the person on the top bunk. Every time they need a book or study materials, they have to climb down, then up the ladder. It's ridiculous. They can keep the TV on the shelf, but not books.

Calendars are another mind numbing issue. The store sells us an 8 x 11 all-on-one sheet calendar that is supposed to serve us to keep track of appointments, classes, medicines, visits, etc. Of course, there is no room to write on it, but in Wonderland, we're supposed to be responsible. Why then aren't inmates allowed to have a proper 12 month calendar or day timer with room to keep track of our lives? Families would love to send these in, but it is not allowed. Why? Because the store sells a calendar, period.

There's a *crazy clothes rule.* When I leave my room early in the morning and the temperature is 48° and drizzling, I'll wear my sweatshirt and coat. When I return from work at two o'clock in the afternoon, it is 85° and warm, but policy says I must wear my sweatshirt and coat regardless of the temperature. I cannot carry them. If I go to a visit when it's chilly and I wear my sweatshirt, I have to keep it on no matter how much it warms up. They say it's a security risk. I sure hope the public feels safer.

Remember the *crazy magazine rule.* I can't tear out an article to send to a friend or a recipe to keep or a picture to put on my bulletin board. If I do, the magazine immediately becomes contraband. One year *TIME's Person of the Year* issue came with a Mylar mirror on the cover.

I can't have the magazine because someone in the mailroom decides that small tissue thin piece of Mylar is a security risk. The mail room officer says I have a choice. I can toss out the issue or mail it out. Just tear off the cover, I plead, so I can read this big double issue. Nope, that will alter it and make it contraband. He finally decides I can use it for my classes as research, and I quickly race out before he can change his mind.

Another uniquely ADC restriction is fruit. They are convinced if inmates are allowed to buy fruit or real fruit juice, we will all immediately be making hooch. If that happens, why not punish the guilty rather than prevent the rest of us from enhancing our extremely limited diet. We are served a Kool-Aid-wanna-be at meals that is sickeningly sweet, and we are sold powdered, presweetened drinks from the store. The dietician had the gall to tell us it's as good as drinking real juice because it is fortified. I figured she was either a terrible dietician or a really good liar.I lobbied for years to sell us V8 juice, but even that is banned and I am desperate for vegetables. Inmates can have all the chips, candy, and cookies they can afford, but nothing healthy is allowed. And yet, all this creates very obese inmates prone to diabetes and heart disease. So what's worse, dealing with a few individuals who try to make hooch, or paying the costly Medical bills related to the diseases caused by obesity?

Being proactive is rare in prison, especially with Medical issues. The majority of the population has some problem with addiction. Drugs and alcohol are definitely forbidden, but another major addiction, smoking, is supported, mainly because the staff is addicted too. There's been a lot of talk about making the prison a non-smoking facility, but they're afraid if they do about a third of the staff will quit.

One of my real pet peeves is the *crazy cigarette rule* that I've mentioned before. I still have a hard time grasping these numbers. Inmates are allowed to buy ten packs of cigarettes, seven packs of chewing tobacco, and twenty-four pouches of rolling tobacco *every week*. They can buy twenty-four sodas, ten candy bars and ten bags of chips *every week*. But we aren't allowed to have healthy snacks. Do you see a pattern here? If you choose, you can smoke yourself to death. We asked them to sell the patch to inmates to help them stop smoking, but got a resounding NO. I'm not trying to begrudge anyone their tobacco and candy, but I wish fruit and books were as readily available. It's a fact — healthy bodies and minds would cost ADC's Medical Department a lot less money in the long run.

Harvard Medical School and other researchers have shown the link between healthy bodies and healthy minds which even in prison could lead to more productive inmates who wouldn't re-offend. Yet, that proactive path is rarely followed. A prison Weight Watcher's program would make a huge impact, but first there would have to be healthy foods available. One Sunday morning's brunch consisted of a biscuit and a cinnamon roll, a ladle of gray gelatinous stuff called sausage gravy (I think the tiny specks were the sausage bits), one-half cup of fried potatoes, one boiled egg, one cup of cheerios, one-quarter cup of canned pineapple, and eight ounces of milk. If you ate all of it, you were guaranteed a food coma.

There are actually acres of fields surrounding most of ADC's prisons that used to be planted with crops. The prisons were self-sufficient and vegetables were plentiful. That was stopped years ago, and now ADC pays out millions of dollars to an outside contractor to feed us terrible meals. Now we get a tissue thin slice of tomato at sixteen meals a year, we never see any kind of squash, and broccoli is very rare. Lots of potatoes though, and always with a weird taste.

ADC policies could fill a room. These are just a few of the nonsensical ones that do more harm than good. Usually I try to laugh them off, so I won't cry. My problem is I try to understand them and ADC operates on the theory that ours is not to reason why. Don't ever question, just obey the rules. That's what an inmate does.

In the real world, people make decisions based on questions and evaluations, and then they take responsibility for their decisions. In prison, making decisions is pretty rare, and yet very important for inmates to learn. A professor told me studies show the average person makes about 6,000 decisions a day; an average inmate makes about 600. When release comes, fear and confusion come with it because the outside world is just one huge Wal-Mart of choices and decisions. The key to surviving and thriving in all of this is patience and a sense of humor. Come to think of it, those qualities will go a long way anywhere . . . *inside or out.*

*The New Republic. www.tnr.com   October 21, 2003

Chapter 24

Summer Hell

August 2005. Summer in Phoenix is like a four-month visit to hell. In the real world, most homes have air-conditioning and the biggest summer challenge is finding a shaded parking place for your car. By mid-July, most people would hock their grandmother for such a spot.

Of course, shady spots are in very short supply so Phoenicians are used to coming back from appointments to a car whose internal temperature is hot enough to bake a cake, with a steering wheel that will give you blisters. I haven't driven a car in years, but the memory was seared into my brain.

Summer in Perryville is magnified by a number too big to count. We are surrounded by fields of dirt and yards of rocks and concrete. Thankfully, the Administration has pity on the staff because the offices and classrooms are air-conditioned, but everything else is cooled (and I use the word loosely) by ancient evap-coolers and fans. Once the temperature hits 90, they are useless. Additionally, the yards are enormous and everywhere inmates go is a substantial hike — in the heat. My body temperature hasn't cooled down in two months. One week, they found me collapsed on the road, dizzy and disoriented. It was the heat.

My first summer at Perryville was almost indescribable. I was going through radiation therapy and my reaction was quite severe. I was blistered and bleeding all across my chest and the heat was stifling. There were no fans then and I was assigned to a particularly hot room. Even the officers refused to come into it. It was an oven. Day after day, I lay in a pool of sweat, trying to hold my t-shirt away from my raw chest. Poor Melissa, my roommate after Gina, tried to comfort me while we suffered together in the heat. It was agony neither of us will ever forget.

My second summer, the Director decided it was indeed unbearably hot and inmates would be allowed to purchase fans. It was August by then and the heat lay over Perryville like a shroud. We were elated over the new ruling and, in our naïveté, we thought the fans would be readily available. Actually, it took nine months for ADC to source out an acceptable clear plastic fan to sell us for $20.90 each. Expensive on our salaries, but everyone scrimped and saved unless their families helped. They finally materialized in April, just in time for the summer's heat. The small plastic fan successfully pushes the hot air around, and if you keep your t-shirt damp, it feels almost cool. Couple that with a *mild* summer of many days below 110° and we were all very grateful.

Then came the *summer of 2005*. As the temperature soared over 115 degrees day after day, tempers flared, inmates collapsed, and life was generally wretched. And it wasn't even mid-July. On Sunday, July 10th, the yard was suddenly locked down. I was at a visit and we watched from across the field as a fire truck and ambulance were allowed on the yard. Later, we learned that a young woman had tried to commit suicide. She was being treated by the Psych Department and was very heavily medicated. At count, she refused to lock down; she said she'd kill herself if they locked her down. They locked her down anyway and she was true to her word. She slashed her throat with her broken light bulb and then attacked her arms. There was an ocean of blood. Only one officer was willing to deal with the blood and tried to help her, holding towels against her throat to stop the flow. In their defense, 25% to 35% of all inmates have Hepatitis C, so no one wants to take that risk. Eventually, she was flown out to the hospital. There was so much blood the room had to be hosed down and lots of things were thrown away.

She lived and returned to Perryville that very night to suicide watch in CDU. I have mixed emotions about that. I've written before of how awful suicide watch is in prison. I believe you must be really desperate to try to kill yourself and when you do, you need love, gentleness, and compassion to recover wholly. There is none forthcoming in prison. The good news is she was moved to the Women's Treatment Unit at Lumley, a very small unit for inmates with severe emotional problems that need constant supervision and medication. There is a long waiting list.

Five days after that drama, we had more. At about 2:30 on

Friday afternoon, July 14th, a young inmate died on our unit at the exact moment Perryville had a massive power failure. As the Medical staff tried to use the defibrillator on her heart, the electricity went off. Imagine the timing. Immediately, the entire yard was emptied as one massive lockdown was announced. At the time, we didn't know about the death, only the power failure.

As the temperature soared to 117 degrees, we were confined to our rooms that effectively became concrete coffins. No power, no circulation. I lay on my bunk in my shorts with two wet washcloths on my head and neck, trying to stay as still as I could. Then I got the brilliant idea of filling an old hair spray bottle with water and spraying my body to help cool it. It helped, a little.

After about three hours of suffocating heat, there was an explosion outside our fence. The generator blew up, filling the air with black smoke. We were all evacuated to the other side of the yard. I grabbed my water and spray bottle and a towel to sit on, found some rare shade and watched the chaos. We were actually very lucky. The C.O.'s assigned to our yard that day were calm and practical. No yelling, no drama. There are a few who love to yell and add to the confusion, but thankfully, they were elsewhere.

In the midst of our misery, the Captain visited every yard to tell us Susie, lovely twenty-five year old Susie, was dead. The heat seemed inconsequential in the face of this news and our misery multiplied. The Captain said those of us wanting to talk to the Chaplain could sign up to see him the next day. For me, it was déjà vu and I signed up. The memory of Gina's death two years ago was still fresh in my mind and this hurt, a lot.

We sat in the heat until about seven in the evening when we were finally fed our supper in the stifling cafeteria. No one had much of an appetite. We felt a bit numb, but as we walked back to our yard, a cheer went up. The power was back. Thank God. I didn't want to spend a whole night locked in those rooms without electricity.

The weekend was a disaster. Emotions were high, but the heat was higher. The officer's radios crackled as first one, then another, and another inmate collapsed. Heat triggers seizures and seizures also trigger more seizures. It's a domino effect. There simply weren't enough officers to cover it all. Meg and I stayed in our little room all weekend trying to stay cool and . . . well, cool isn't the right word.

Trying to stay tepid is more like it. It was a very bad time and I was thankful for my books, my TV, and electricity. I was thankful once again to be alive.

The aftermath of that weekend was palpable. We could all feel the tension and there was no escaping the ongoing heat. Nevertheless, we had a couple of weeks of near normalcy. Relief spread over us. Then on Tuesday, August 2nd, we awoke to a massive lockdown. Our quarterly shake, three weeks early. It was a long day. Locked down fourteen hours. Rooms in disarray; not to mention lining up in the heat against the fence so the K-9 could sniff us. In the time I was at Perryville, I never heard of staff finding any drugs that way, but you never know. We were all glad to see the end of that day. Three months until the next one.

That evening, I sat down to write a letter to my husband and noticed the paper was suddenly gritty. I brushed it off. More grit. In an instant, I realized what it was and dashed to the window. The world looked like a tornado of dark brown dust swirling around furiously, filling up our room, bed, clothes, hair, everything. We felt like we were eating dust sandwiches. When it was finally over, Meg and I cleaned off every surface and our beds before we went to sleep, but the floor had to wait until the next day.

To our great dismay, we awoke to another lockdown. What now? Can't be another shake. Nope, it's a water failure. No water in all of Perryville. That means no cleaning, no showers, no *flushing*. This was not good. Once again, we were locked down all day except for the field trips (literally across the field) to the port-a-johns. That day felt like a week. Finally about 4:00 in the afternoon, we got enough water pressure to flush. Still no showers, but the flushing was a blessing. However, the rumors flew that the crisis would go on through the weekend. Those pesky rumors again; they multiply faster than rabbits, and I was praying that's all they were — rumors.

Thursday morning we were still locked down, but at 5:40, our C.O. came to tell me I had fifteen minutes to get ready for a surprise trip to Maricopa Medical Center. I asked for a shower. There's a little water pressure. No shower allowed. I protested. *But I'm going to see the doctor.* No shower. So I have a birdbath in the sink, throw on my clothes, gulp a little food, and dash up front to wait. I haven't done this trip in two years, but it never changes. Shackles, handcuffs, sack lunch, dirty holding tanks. Another long day.

This was for a bone density test, a test I've been requesting for two years. Because of my Medical history, I'm at high risk of osteoporosis. I learned at the hospital that nearly 50% of American women over fifty have it. The good news is there are fantastic new meds to build bones and give hope to millions.

There was more good news. I got back to the prison in time for lunch. It was tomato day! I got the paper-thin slice of tomato that is on the menu every three weeks and it was wonderful. And the good news kept coming. Water was back to normal. I could shower off the grime of the hospital trip, rest a bit, and cool off. It was a full three weeks.

I tried to clear my mind and feel the peace of meditation. I'd been trying that all during the past three weeks, but my mind would not clear. My thoughts fluttered around, banging into the sides of my brain, giving me no rest. Daily life behind bars is always unsettling. You never know when an officer in a bad mood will decide to ruin your day so you are ever on your guard. Then with crisis after crisis in that brief three-week period, everyone was just worn out.

In the midst of this, I remembered something Charles Swindell said,

> *"The only thing we can do is play on the one string we have, and that is our attitude . . . I am convinced that life is 10% what happens to me, and 90% how I react to it. And so it is with you . . . we are in charge of our attitudes."*

It's that pesky word again — *choice*. Nowhere is that quote more obvious than in prison. Despite the horrible heat, the lock downs, the water shortage, and the shake, we always have a choice. It's the one thing we can control. Some people choose to stress over the craziness of Wonderland. I choose peace, quiet, and optimism, good things to choose . . . *inside or out.*

Chapter 25

Attitude

September 2005. I coined a new acronym — WIGO. It stands for *When I Get out*. When I Get Out I'm going to get a job. When I Get Out I'm going to be a blonde, I'm going to hug my kids, I'm going to Vegas and my life will be perfect. Isn't that just like outside? When I get a job, when I get a raise, when I get married, when I lose weight, then my life will be perfect. We're always waiting for **LIFE** to happen. We all have dreams, plans, and possibilities for our perfect future.

So what do we do until all our dreams come true? A lot of inmates wish that, like Sleeping Beauty, they could take one huge sleeping pill at R & A and wake up at the end of their sentence because freedom is the ultimate dream come true. A lot of people outside are like that too; people wishing their lives away. For many, they find numbness and escape in drugs. They literally sleepwalk through their lives. Whenever I ask what attracted them to drugs, nine times out of ten, it's numbness.

Prison is a perfect example of wishing time away. Everyone has a different approach to doing time. First, there are the hardcore inmates who come in mad at the world and ready to fight at the drop of a hat. Their vision of life is from the streets — survival of the fittest, don't be a wimp, "I can lick you any day." They sit on the yards, rain or shine (in Arizona it's mostly shine), smoking, swearing, and criticizing what's wrong with the world, the prison, the officers, and the other inmates. They don't have any solutions, but they are world champs in criticizing.

Occasionally, they flex their muscles with a fight. With the men, it's usually a quick one round that the C.O.'s don't even see. With the women, it's more flailing of arms and hair-pulling with maybe a lucky bite or scratch. Everybody gets hauled off to The Hole to cool off for a week or two or, if it's really serious, six months. One young woman spent the first two years of her prison life in The Hole with intermittent weeks of freedom in general population. Her anger was incredibly deep and she was determined to be pissed off.

Outside there are people like that too, mad at the world. Mostly they sit in bars smoking and swearing and bitching about what's wrong with the world, their job, their boss, and their spouse. They won't make a move to change things, like maybe their attitude, but how they can moan. And just like inside, they even pick an occasional fight to feed their anger, determined to be pissed off too.

After the hardcore troublemakers, there are the time wasters. They don't fight. They don't even get in much trouble, but, oh, how they waste time. Somehow they manage to avoid any idea of a job, sitting on their bunks, watching endless TV (bought with their families' hard earned cash).

There are also the champion card players, any game, anytime. The card players usually team up with the hard-core smokers. Smoke, TV, cards, the great prison and the great American pass times. Outside the same type of people wish their lives away, wasting time living by the WIG creed: *When I Get a job,* a husband, a house, a new figure, my life will be *perfect.* Meanwhile, I'll just waste my time away with drugs or alcohol or video games or shopping.

Finally, there are those inmates who scurry to get a job, join programs, sign up for school, and go to church. Candace was that way. She worked a 40-hour week from four in the morning until noon at the Print Shop. She'd stumble off her upper bunk at 3:15, splash water on her face, and slide into the dreaded orange outfit we came to hate. Candace had to be at the gate by 3:30 to sit and wait until she was allowed to pass through at four.

At noon, after work, she would sit in a cage in the hot sun with no shade for up to an hour, waiting for an officer to be available to conduct the strip-search before the inmates could return to the yard, just in case anyone was tempted to steal a paperclip or a rubber band. Once through the gate, she'd race to her one o'clock class in Parenting or Graphic Arts. At four, she'd dash back to the yard for count, gulp her dinner, then hurry to another class or program from five to eight. It was a killer pace, but Candace was determined to make the most of her time. In seven months, she accomplished more than most inmates do in years. Candace left prison with no home, car, or clothes, but I have no doubt she will succeed.

So what's the big difference? It's that old Charles Swindoll quote again about attitude. In prison we aren't in charge of much. We're told when and how to do everything. It's nice to realize we can control something, something so important, so powerful it impacts our life, our family, our job, our community, even our world. Look how one terrorist's desire to kill, like Osama Bin Laden, can destroy so much and how one man's desire to forgive, like Nelson Mandela, can change a country.

Often people take drugs because they feel like they're nothing, nobody, with no hope, no future. That's a negative attitude. But think of the nobodies who've impacted the world. Mother Teresa, Martin Luther King, Jr., Corrie ten Boom, Helen Keller, Gandhi, Oprah — all *nobodies with a positive attitude*. The gunmen at Columbine High School tried to destroy a community with their attitude. The community has not allowed that. They too have attitude — strong, positive, faith-based attitude. Who are they? They're nobodies, but *nobodies with the right attitude*.

It's the same with us. We're all nobodies, but with the right attitude, we too can make a difference. When you realize that, you'll take charge of your life and stop waiting for the WIGO creed to happen. Then you will be the one to make a difference whether you are . . . *inside or out*.

Chapter 26

Money in Prison

October 2005. Money in prison has a meaning and value that is totally contrary to the real world. Inmates have jobs. Well, some do. Those that have jobs make a salary. There is even a store for shopping. And, like outside, they have expenses. That all sounds familiar, but that's where the familiarity stops. In prison, money takes on a whole new meaning.

ADC wants the public to believe every inmate has something productive to do with their time, but over the years more and more jobs have been taken away and now there are very few left of meaning. Inmates used to act as secretaries and clerks to help alleviate the over-worked staff. Now, however, inmates aren't even allowed to answer phones, make copies, or type. There even used to be a farm where inmates could learn agricultural husbandry and the prison could be self-sufficient in the dining rooms, but that was stopped years ago.

The list of approved jobs is very limited. The few jobs that let inmates use their brains are called clerks, Program Clerks, Women in Recovery clerks, State Issue and Store clerks, Counselor clerks and Chaplain's clerks. There are also Teacher's Aides who actually do all the teaching while the civilian teachers supervise. These jobs total about forty on a yard with nearly 800 women. Everything else is manual labor, including the floor crew, kitchen workers, supply clerks, shower and pod porters, office porters, visitation porters, yard crew and outside landscaping. It all involves cleaning or in the case of yard crew, raking rocks. Yes, there really is a job to keep the rocks neat and tidy.

For all these jobs, pay ranges from 10¢ to 45¢ an hour. Gosh, who makes 45¢? Must be the Teacher's Aids, right? Nope. They start at 30¢. It's the floor crew. That requires skilled labor, but teaching doesn't, in ADC's mind anyway, although Teacher's Aid is the only job that requires a score of 12/9 on the scholastic admission's test.

There are also a limited amount of jobs that start at 45¢ and go up to $1 working in the Garment Factory, the Print Shop, or outside landscaping crews in townships around the prison, like Goodyear. And there is a tele-marketing company that pays minimum wage for a very select group of about two hundred of the 3,600 at Perryville. Those women are fortunate enough to actually build up a nest egg for their release.

I've had several jobs. Initially, I was a Teacher's Aid, but daily trips to the hospital for radiation interfered, so I became the Chaplain's clerk, a position I held for two years. Nice job, pleasant atmosphere, and 30¢ an hour. ADC policy states that inmates are supposed to get a 5¢ an hour pay raise every six months until they reach the 50¢ ceiling. However, when I arrived, they told me all wages were frozen so it took me two years to get a nickel raise. Then I became a Peer Educator at 35¢ and then back to Teacher's Aid, this time focused on GED. It took me six years to work up to 45¢ despite what policy said. In the meantime, my husband was also a Teacher's Aide and I learned that the wages on the men's yards were never frozen.

The gist is, no one has any money. But why would an inmate need any money? Doesn't the prison provide everything? Sort of. As a new inmate, you get three T- shirts, two pair of trousers, three pair of socks, panties and bras, one winter jacket, one baseball cap, and one pair of boots. Also, two sheets, one lumpy pillow and pillow case (a luxury after the jail), two very thin towels, and three washcloths. That's called State Issue. And, after all, what else does a girl need?

ADC also allows a sweatshirt and sweatpants for winter and shorts for summer, but you have to buy them. It's a pretty cold winter for the women who can't afford a sweatshirt and summers are beyond miserable without shorts. If you have no family or outside support, life is much more difficult and the isolation increases one hundred fold.

Additionally, ADC allows inmates to purchase a pair of sneakers by Nike or New Balance at a captive cost of $48. A deal outside, but on an inmate's salary, it's pretty steep. The option is wearing the very stiff blister-maker work boots made in China. The yards are very spread out and we can walk miles in a day so understandably the first thing an inmate asks her family to do is send money to buy the sneakers.

ADC is supposed to replace worn out clothes quarterly, but generally you just get someone else's less worn, faded, holey orange stuff. Fortunately, ADC also sells new T-shirts and trousers as well as panties, bras, and socks. More reasons for money. Clothes wear out fast in prison, especially since we wear the same stuff every day. Our sheets and towels are only replaced if they look like Swiss cheese and we aren't allowed to buy extras. Owning four sheets and three or four towels would be just too much luxury.

That covers our whimsically named State Issue. But what about hygiene needs? Each inmate is issued one roll of tissue-thin toilet paper a week and if you run out, too bad. I did run out in R & A and, in my naïveté, I went to the officer to ask for more. He paused, looked at me and snapped, "No."

I was stunned. After all, toilet paper is a pretty basic human need and we aren't a third world country.

"But what shall I do?" I implored.

He sneered as he looked down on me like I was an insect and raised his eyebrow,

"It sucks to be you."

If you run out of toilet paper, we are allowed to buy Charmin at 74¢ a roll which adds up to about two and a half hours work at 30¢ an hour. We are also issued fifteen sanitary pads a month. If you need more or want tampax, they are for sale.

The State provides nothing else unless you are indigent. That means you have less than $12 a month in your inmate account. An indigent inmate gets a small amount of the poorest quality soap, deodorant, toothpaste, a comb, shampoo, shaving cream, and a razor replaced when you run out. Anything else is considered a luxury. If friends and family didn't help, you would do without chap sticks, vitamins, Vaseline, hand lotion, eye drops, aspirin, Band-Aids, conditioner, sunscreen, a hair brush, paper, a pen, stamps, envelopes, mouthwash, denture cream, Q-tips, the very basics that you take for granted on the outside. These are not State Issue.

There are also luxuries, like a clock, a radio/tape player, a TV, a few arts and crafts supplies, and the most precious of all, an electric fan that cools your rooms down to 90° in the summer and also serves to dry both hair and clothes.

Budgeting to buy the basic needs is tough. Consider that many of the women here make 10¢ an hour and usually only get to work twenty hours a week. That's $2 a week. ADC takes 25% or 50¢ until they've collected $50. Remember Candace? That's your Gate Fee and is returned to you upon release. Supposedly it's your nest egg to help you reintegrate into society, but in reality, what's $50 going to cover? Maybe a meal and bus fare.

So an inmate makes $1.50 a week or $6 a month. That makes her indigent and eligible for basic State Issue hygiene. As soon as she gets an increase to 20¢ an hour, her salary is now $12 a month and she is no longer eligible for the indigent package. She now has to buy her own hygiene out of $3 a week. If she drinks coffee, wants to send a letter or have a little snack, not a chance. Additionally, if she's here for a DUI, 60% of her salary is deducted for Mothers Against Drunk Driving. Those women truly do work for pennies and find it impossible to live without outside family support. This 60% deduction penalizes both the inmate and the family. I understand the money is supposed to go to programming for alcoholism, but in my seven years I never heard of one program funded by MADD. It's a great idea; I'd just like to see it happen.

Here's where the underground economy kicks in. The women who work for minimum wage are the most affluent in the community. They can afford to buy new clothes and prefer not to send their clothes to the ADC laundry because they come back dingy grey, damp, and smelly. They pay enterprising young women to wash their clothes at a going rate of 50¢ an item. Of course, no money changes hands. Inmates aren't allowed to touch money. The currency is in items from the store.

There are others who are quite artistic and make a prison living making greeting cards, using the paltry selection of art supplies sold from the store. They sell for one to three dollars, depending on the quality. Either enterprise is highly illegal. Bartering and trading are serious infractions and can result in a major ticket. However, the officers generally turn a blind eye if they see any laundry drying or greeting cards lying about. They know if they really stopped it, the whole prison economy would collapse, the store would lose money, and there would be more inmates getting indigent packets out of ADC's budget.

So you see, prison can be quite expensive for an inmate and a burden for her family. Just for the basics, money really is important. Jobs are critical to keep an inmate busy, allow her to pay her way, and prepare her for her release. Unfortunately, ADC is failing in that regard, one of the reasons recidivism is so high. I'd take an educated guess that 80% of those released are woefully unprepared for employment or life. The system has become a squirrel cage overloaded with too many entries and too few releases. Currently ADC releases 19,000 inmates a year and admits 21,000. Job security is alive and well.

When it comes to employment, I am really blessed. I've always held a job. The State takes 30% of my salary for restitution, leaving me about $9 a week on which to live. I am also blessed to have friends who send me money on holidays and special occasions. That allows me to buy things like shoes and clothes. It also allowed me to buy my radio, clock, fan, and television, for which my gratitude knows no bounds. Otherwise, I would have a stifling hot room with neither news nor music.

There is a bright spot to living on a shoe string. It teaches us a true appreciation for every tiny thing. I've learned what I can live without and any treat I get is a true delight. In this world of consumerism and stuff, that's a good lesson to learn . . . *inside or out.*

Chapter 27

Curiosity

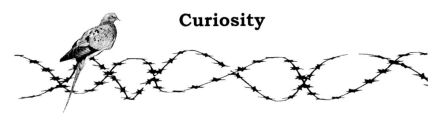

March 2006. Curiosity is a powerful tool for life. Of all my many prison roommates, the one that stands out in my mind is Elizabeth for her incredible lack of curiosity. She also lacked vision and dreams. I've come to believe they all go hand in hand.

Elizabeth was only 23 when she was assigned to my room. When she moved in, I could read her mind. *Oh, no! Not that old lady.*

Moreover, my thoughts are equally prejudicial. *Oh, no! Not that child.*

Neither of us thinks it is a match made in heaven. After all, she is still struggling with getting her mandatory eighth grade certificate. What on earth will we talk about?

First, I encourage her to pass her mandatory. I soon learn that she isn't stupid, just undisciplined and a tad lazy. She'd much rather play cards in the smoking section than study. But I keep encouraging her and quite soon she passes. Then I sign her up for GED tutoring. She protests, loudly. She doesn't need a GED.

"Well, you signed me up so I might as well go."

Only six weeks later, she passes and is excited beyond words. I know she surprised herself.

"OK, now you need to go to Rio Salado." Again she protests, loudly. She doesn't need Rio. I sign her up anyway.

"Well, you signed me up so I might as well go." One by one, she passes her levels and feels proud to be a "college girl."

All through the year we lived together, I ask about her dreams and ambitions. She doesn't have any beyond cards and cigarettes. Remarkably incurious about life, she can't see herself beyond the gates of Perryville. However, eventually she is released, and I hear through the grapevine that she's been hired by a local resort to work at the front desk. She sent word that she owed it all to me, but she did the work. I just signed her up.

There are too many like Elizabeth. They have no vision beyond the card table in the smoking section and no curiosity about life. Once I asked a neighbor if she'd ever been to Sedona. She looked at me blankly. She'd never been out of west Phoenix. Forget Sedona. She hadn't been to Mesa or Scottsdale. She told me how incredibly restricted her life was, even before prison. She was in other type of prison, one without bars. So many of them were shackled by poverty, abusive families, addiction, and lack of education. It was hard enough to get to school; Sedona was like going to the moon. They learned to numb their feelings and their curiosity.

In my job as GED tutor, I deal with this lack of curiosity daily. Prison is an opportunity to use this time to really learn. To pass the GED, they have to study not only math, reading, and language, but social studies and science as well. When I was in fifth grade, I had the most wonderful teacher named Mrs. Poole. It didn't matter what we were talking about, Mrs. Poole would go to her cupboards and dig around. Eventually, she would pull out a small bottle of sand from the pyramids or photographs from the Grand Canyon. She did her best to make history and geography come alive for us and it worked. I'll never forget her. For me, she defined teaching. It's making things come alive and relevant to incurious and often bored students.

Here, with very limited resources, I do my best to imitate Mrs. Poole. Despite the fact that I am creating contraband, I save magazine articles and pictures. I scrounge books. I want to introduce them to all kinds of new ideas and wonders, even behind bars. Especially behind bars. But I'm sad when some only want to learn the very basics to pass with the lowest grade possible. No curiosity. No vision. Just get it over with.

I try to recall what I was like at 23 or even 33. Did I want to just get by? I don't remember that. I do remember an insatiable curiosity. I wanted to see the world and I always wanted to know **why**. I had dreams and vision but I wasn't shackled by my surroundings like these young women were. Now I have different dreams. The old ones were all about me and how I could climb the ladder of success. After all, I started my career path in the 70's when we were all supposed to be Wonder Woman. Now I dream of how I can be of service and help this forgotten population I've been a part of for so long.

This is an incredible journey. It's hard, sometimes devastatingly so, but it enriches my life in countless ways, through the people and the situations. My motto now is . . .

Been there.
Done that.
Now how can I help?

I'm still curious, I'm still learning, and I encourage those qualities in everyone. Be curious, learn, and help, good qualities to have . . . *inside or out.*

Chapter 28

Direct Orders and Etiquette

April 2006. Some days prison feels like adult day care, (hence the ADC) and other times I am reminded that it is indeed a real prison. Most of the time the *girls* act like it's one big slumber party, albeit from hell, and other times, it's no slumber party. It's just hell.

Recently, one of the old numbers doing *Life on the instalment plan* (you know, five years in, two years out; six years in, three years out), got a major ticket, and was reclassed to Lumley. Lumley is the maximum security yard. Lots less recreation, much more cell time. Nobody wants to go there, but Jewel is told she's on her way.

"You cannot pack your stuff. You cannot tell your sister, Sunny, goodbye. You cannot pass Go . . . just proceed directly to the sally port to wait for transportation."

Jewel heard this and made up her own mind where she was going. When she left the office, instead of turning left, she turned right and went down to the picnic tables where Sunny was waiting to hear the news. These sisters are very close and determined to say goodbye if the worst is confirmed.

In prison lingo, that right turn meant *disobeying a direct order* and is absolutely **forbidden**. Hot on Jewel's trail are a C.O.II and a lieutenant who are yelling at her to cease and desist.

"No way. Not 'til I hug my sister."

This is like waving a red flag at a bull. Officers feel their authority is being threatened and are always afraid they'll look foolish. SWAT team mentality kicks in. They start screaming and threatening.

"Stop hugging that inmate. Get your hands off her. Now! Now! Get on the ground. Down! Down! Now! NOW!"

It's as if they are screaming at a dog and, like any frisky dog, Jewel is not listening. Well, that's not entirely true. She hears and her response is a whole string of words, mostly beginning with the letter F. By now, everybody is yelling. Officers are running in every direction, and there is a wall of orange all lined up to watch. The first C.O. is threatening pepper spray.

On my way to work, I walk right by as the yelling starts, my sign to get the heck out of Dodge. Officers hate for inmates to witness any of these dramas because they might actually become unfavorable witnesses. However, in their defense, the policy now is to video tape everything. In this case, the C.O. with the camera isn't there yet, and all eyes are glued to these two women hugging in the center of the field.

Suddenly the C.O. makes good his threat, despite the cooler head of the lieutenant who warns him to back off. The pepper spray flies and there is more yelling, interspersed with very loud sobbing from Sunny, as Jewel, the tougher of the two, tries to comfort her.

The spraying C.O. is actually sent back to the yard office at the lieutenant's direction as the two inmates are surrounded by a gang of staff. No one, however, is trying to touch them or to subdue them. That can result in being scratched, bitten, or spit on so the C.O.'s are keeping a healthy distance, out of spit range, but still herding them like lost sheep up toward the offices.

It's working and they are quieter. The yelling stops, although Sunny is sobbing from the pepper spray. By now, I am up at my workstation at the Chaplain's office in Visitation and can watch safely from a distance behind glass. Then the C.O. orders all the inmates outside into the visitation area out of the way, and about fifty gawking orange pumpkins move inside, each eager for a look, but hampering my view.

Suddenly, as they round the corner, *Officer Pepper Spray* walks out of the yard office to join the crowd. When Jewel sees him, she tries to break free to charge in his direction. Sunny tries to hold her back. Sunny is not the only one. Several other officers tackle her like the Dallas Cowboys and all we see are arms and legs flailing away. It is a real mêlée, escalated by SWAT tactics, and ending with a pile of bodies, orange and brown.

At last we hear the clinking, jingling sound of handcuffs and shackles that are used to subdue both sisters. One is finally led away, but the other has to be carried off on a stretcher. There is a lot of blood and the staff is very anxious that the blood be cleaned up immediately. All the gawkers are sent back to their cells for lockdown.

After an incident like this, there are briefings to make sure all the stories are straight, followed by reams of reports of be filed. I am still up in the art room by Visitation with the other inmates who work there. In the excitement, we are overlooked and we are all keeping our heads down, reading or painting, anxious to stay out of the way. Finally we see one of the sisters ushered out in chains. They literally hose her down to wash off the pepper spray and bring her back soaked like a bad dog.

The briefings and comments by the Deputy Warden last a couple of hours, and finally all is normal again except for the gossip. Well, that's normal too. I am fascinated listening to the stories. According to *brown* (what the officers wear), they disobeyed a direct order; they got what they deserved; all force was necessary to quell the disturbance. According to *orange* (what the inmates wear), all she wanted to do was say goodbye to her sister.

Somewhere in all the pages of reports, I hope an astute administrator realizes there has to be a better way. Maybe I'm naïve, but this SWAT team aggression seems to escalate the anger and confusion. Nobody had a gun, yet these inmates were treated like they were armed and dangerous. Yes, she *disobeyed a direct order*. Is bloodshed necessary? Why not just write her the major ticket as she says goodbye to her sister and lead her away to The Hole? Punish her, don't make a brawl out of it.

There are some people who come to work in a prison because they genuinely think they can make a positive difference in the lives of inmates. There are some who sign up for the benefits package and job security. They just punch a clock and hope nothing ever happens on their shift. Others like the whole paramilitary structure. They can't get into the Army for any number of reasons, so they join the *prison army* and find a home. They are on a definite power trip. They see inmates as the dregs of humanity, dogs to be caged and bullied until release date.

In the *Stanford Prison Project* (a landmark experiment about incarceration), Philip Zimbardo discovered that the more aggressive guards (actually college students who were part of the experiment) held more influence over the more humane guards (also college students) who feared being seen as wimpy and weak instead of agents for positive change. His powerful book, *The Lucifer Effect*, is a fascinating and in-depth study of this behavior.

Unfortunately, because the system is dehumanizing, the aggressive guards succeed far more than the humane ones. That's the tragedy. When you treat a human being with cruelty, you're going to end up with an angry, hostile human and that often happens in prison.

Inmates are not taught how to behave in polite society or in the business world. Policy states we can't even be called by a respectful title. Inmate Allen or simply Allen is allowed, but no form of courtesy like Ms. Allen is permitted. There actually are officers who disobey the rule and address me politely as Ms. Allen and I bless them silently for their dignity and simple good manners. What kind of person dreams up such a dehumanizing policy? It is a small, demeaning symbol of ADC's mentality, that inmates aren't people anymore.

I used to think I was just old-fashioned. Maybe the rules of etiquette don't apply anymore. Then a friend gave me a subscription to Glamour magazine and I was blown away. Initially I thought I was too old for Glamour, but the quality of their article surprised me. They aim at a Yuppie woman seeking advice and enlightenment about business, politics, and the economy as well as the old standby's, fashion and sex. Basically, I learned I'm not that old-fashioned. The rules of etiquette still do apply: things like civility, thank you notes, handshakes, and calling someone Ms. Jones.

So what is the lesson in all this drama? Good manners are never out of style. Children are like sponges and what they learn at a young age stays with them and contributes to their success or failure. It's monkey see, monkey do. If you're rude, abusive, swear like a sailor, break the rules, do drugs, drive while drinking (I'm not just talking here about inmates), your child will model that behavior. That can lead them to prison, and unfortunately, children of inmates have a 63% chance of serving time too. We're all role models and we all have a chance to impact the lives of others . . . *inside or out.*

Chapter 29

Telephones

July 2006. Aren't telephones wonderful? This tiny, miraculous instrument connects you with everyone important in your life — parents, children, spouse, doctor, lawyer, Indian chief. I wonder if Alexander Graham Bell knew he was creating an instrument that would connect the world.

When I was born in 1945, the telephone in our house was black, in the hallway, and calls went through an operator. When we moved to the jungles of Venezuela, there were no phones and we felt like we were on another planet. In 1950, we moved again, to Europe. Phones weren't common in the small French village where we lived, but we had one. Calling my grandmother in Texas was an annual event to which we all looked forward. It was a complicated process of multiple operators and fuzzy conversation. We envisioned the Trans Atlantic cable surrounded by fish nibbling on it while they listened in.

Gradually, telephones found their way into every room in the house. They came in a rainbow of colors and shapes. Remember the Princess phone? The Mickey Mouse phone? Then the cell phone revolution hit and our lives were changed forever. Now people walk around with tiny phones seemingly glued to their heads. Everyone has a phone, even kids in grammar school. Everyone except inmates.

Prison is designed to separate inmates from the world. Some prisons do that better than others. ADC is an expert in separation. We are very limited in who we are allowed to call — only the same ten people who are on the inmate's visitation list. The process for approval is lengthy and time consuming. First, the inmate sends the application to the friend or family member who wants to visit. The applicant must return the completed form to the Visitation Officer for processing. It then takes ADC about two months to run the background checks for approval. Bear in mind that the inmate can spend up to three months in R & A waiting for a bed in general population.

When I entered Perryville, we were not allowed to start the process in R & A. We had to wait until we got to our assigned yard, so it actually could take four to five months before a new inmate was allowed to talk to their children, parent, or spouse. I felt this was unduly harsh, especially at a time when children really need that connection with their parent, a connection that is particularly fragile in prison. Consider that many prisons allow inmates to call anyone collect; the only restriction depends on the party accepting the charges. That seems more fair and allows for families to stay better connected.

Eventually the inmate gets on the yard and starts the process. One bright day, she gets a notice that her family has been approved to visit. Now she has to fill out another form to add them to the formal visitation list, better known as the *Ten List*. That takes more paper and about ten more days. Then she has to fill out yet another form to add the names to her phone list before she is allowed to call them. By now the forests are in serious danger from the volumes of paper required. Naturally everything is in triplicate.

Now, depending on her security level, an inmate is restricted in the number of calls she can make each week. Maximum Security levels are allowed one weekly call. Medium Security levels get four calls. I started at Medium Security and worked my way down to a Minimum Security level so I finally get fourteen calls per week. I'm lucky if I make two but the option is there.

Since ninety-three percent of all inmates are eventually released, why keep them so separated from their families? It's an Arizona thing. Federal prisons allow unlimited collect calls. Some even sell phone cards so the inmate can actually pay for their own calls. But ADC Administration prefers to separate. Rehabilitation is a distant dream.

One week was particularly frustrating for me. I had made two phone calls of the fourteen allowed. Nevertheless, when I tried to call a friend on the weekend, the annoying recorded message advised me that I had exceeded my limit. "What? No, I haven't. I've only made two calls, both on Tuesday." Of course, I realize I am talking to a machine and am absolutely helpless. No one in the entire prison on the weekend can do anything about an inmate's phone problem. It's way down there on the totem pole.

So I wait until Monday. The phones are supposed to reset on Sunday night. First thing Monday morning, I check the phones. That same annoying voice tells me that I've exceeded my limit. "No, I haven't," I tell her, but that is wasted breath. ADC's procedure is to fill out another form and submit it to my counselor. I would but, as usual, he isn't here so I can't even get a form. I have a scheduled call to my friend Diane at nine o'clock on Tuesday so I am particularly motivated to get this rectified.

I go up to the Program Office at 8:30 A.M. to see if I can find anyone to help me. No, they're all in the morning meeting. I wait. An hour and a half later, they're out of their meeting and I'm brushed off with "Go see your counselor. I don't do phones." I trudge back across the yard in the blistering heat to square one.

Finally, a compassionate C.O. III actually listens to me and gets me the proper form. By now, it is time for eleven o'clock count so he tells me to return it after lunch. I do and it's back to waiting. Inmates are not allowed to go into the Program Office without an appointment so I stand outside in the 110 degree heat, waiting for someone to acknowledge me. They can see me through the windows, but officers are experts at ignoring inmates. I wait forty-five minutes in the brutal heat, sitting on a sort of pedestal until the lieutenant walks by and barks, "Allen, you can't sit there." (Staff can, but inmates cannot.) This reminds me again of the ADC policy that prevents officers from calling me Ms. Allen. I long for good manners.

My request to the good Samaritan C.O.III was for either the phones to be fixed or I be given an emergency phone call. Finally he comes out. He went to bat for me, and I must now wait for a decision. More waiting as it gets hotter. I start to recognize the nausea and dizziness that comes with heat exhaustion. I know I have to go back to my room and stand in front of my fan. Last summer, I collapsed three times in the heat and I know the signs.

About an hour later, I hear from my C.O. III that my request has been denied. They have no idea how long before my phone access is fixed, but they are *addressing* it. Despite the fact that it's ADC's fault, my appointment means nothing, and I have no way of reaching Diane so she won't worry. I'm just denied a phone call.

An emergency phone call is for death or critical illness. I could live with that if it were true, but I know my C.O. III doles out emergency phone calls to his favorites for nothing remotely critical. Just like outside, on the inside it's who you know and this time, I'm not on the favored list.

Outside in the free world, you are too often tied to your cell phone and just wish it would stop ringing. Inside, inmates know that connections are precious. The ability to communicate over that visionary instrument created by Mr. Bell is priceless and you only realize it when it's taken away. Connections are a good thing, keeping us motivated, encouraged, and loved, things we all need . . . *inside or out.*

Chapter 30

Colonoscopy Cocktail Party

June 06. You haven't lived until you've had a colonoscopy in the slammer. Seven months ago, the oncologist at Maricopa Medical Center recommended that I have one because of my age and past cancer. ADC Medical responds to such orders with all the speed of a Galapagos turtle and, finally, I am called to Medical to be briefed on the procedure.

I'm surprised to learn the prep takes two days. I know from friends outside that their prep only took a day so I ask why. "Because most inmates don't follow instructions and when they get to the hospital, they aren't clean enough and the procedure can't be done. That just wastes time and money and annoys everyone." Of course, I do follow instructions perfectly, but never mind, two days it is.

On Day One, I'm to drink a half gallon of liquid euphemistically called "Golytely" and must stay close to the toilet. They've even written a chrono ordering that. The word is already out that tomorrow is Shake Day, the quarterly search and invasion into our stuff. We can't be in the room when it's being shook. What to do?

First I go to the most reasonable lieutenant to tell her about my condition, but she won't be here tomorrow. She takes me to the first shift lieutenant, another female with all the grace, charm, and compassion of a guard at Abu Ghraib. She's quick to decide I'll have to be locked in an iso cell all day. An iso (isolation) cell is a stark, steel room (with a steel bunk and a toilet) designed to keep problem inmates in check. So to isolate me during this uncomfortable prep, without even a mattress to lie on, would really be inhumane. I must have looked stricken because the first lieutenant said they'd think about it. I fled back to Medical to plead my case.

"Please allow me to stay in my room or just outside during the time that my cell is being searched." I really feel desperate; iso cells are horrible.

Good news. They tell me I don't start the cocktail until noon and if the search starts with 20 Yard, we'll be finished by then. Back to the lieutenant with my news.

"Fine," she says. "We'll be finished with 20 Yard by noon." My relief is palpable.

I spend the evening preparing for the Shake and have my last food for two days. Tuesday dawns, and by eight o'clock., the team has started with D pod on our yard. By nine, we hear the call:

"C pod, line up."

By 9:45, it's all over and our room hasn't been touched. Of course, we don't have anything to hide, but it's still stressful. By eleven, all is back to normal and I'm psyching myself up for the colonoscopy cocktail party at noon.

The drink is mildly salty and unpleasant, but not horrible. The liquid diet the kitchen sends is much worse. The broth is so salty that I gag and throw it down the sink. The Jell-O is liquid. They added water to it, but failed to chill it. How can you mess up Jell-O? Well, at least the tea is nice, but if all I have for two days is tea, it's going to be a long two days.

Did I mention that I also have four laxative tablets to take with the cocktail — eight over two days? Medical must know this is bad because they even give me an extra roll of toilet paper, a commodity here more scarce than a tulip in the desert.

I make it through the afternoon and evening, pretending I'm not hungry. TV has nothing but gorgeous food ads. The next morning I'm back at Medical to get my second container of Golytely. This time, I have to drink the whole gallon. Ugh. I start at noon. I drink and fantasize about food. I'm so hungry. By now, the kitchen is chilling the Jell-O so my diet consists of tea, orange Jell-O, and Golytely. Since I'm hypoglycemic, this isn't great, but I'm determined to do it right and be properly prepped.

Tuesday I'm up at 4:30 in the morning when the doors grind open. I've made over fifty trips to the hospital so I know Transportation usually comes between 6 and 6:30, but the yard officers always start yelling to be ready by 5:30. It's nerve-wracking and I prefer not to go through the yelling. I shower, dress, and wait.

I'm ready. Nothing. At 6:30, I decide to go up to Medical to check things out, but nobody knows where the transportation officers are. They're usually here by now. No one will call and inquire. They just look at me and shrug. *It's not their job.*

I wait until 8:30 and tell the Medical officer I'm going back to my room.

"No, you can't. They'll be here any minute."

I wait another hour in the cage, sitting on the hard concrete bench. Until I came to prison, I never realized how unforgiving concrete is on every part of my body. Finally, I get permission to return to my room, but still no one feels compelled to call Transportation despite my pleadings. I've had a lot of experience with Transportation, and they have been known to make a mistake. Maybe they didn't get the order. I can't bear the idea of missing the appointment and having to do this all over again.

I go back and wait some more. Anxious and ravenous, at 10:30 I walk up again and finally the Medical officer takes pity on me. This is irregular so she makes a call. Turns out my appointment is for 12:30, but as an inmate I'm not supposed to know. I might call someone and plot an escape. Oh, good grief. It would have been lovely to sleep in and relax instead of being ready before dawn cracked.

Finally, Transportation is here and I'm thankful that it's two of the nicest officers on the team. The trip to the hospital is peaceful and the staff is ready for me.

One of the nurses was actually on the staff at Santa Cruz for about a year and she remembers me. She was one of the nicest nurses, but one day she was gone. I ask her why she left. Were the inmates mean? Was she afraid?

"On the contrary," she says. "The inmates were fine, but I felt so frustrated. There was so little we could do to help because ADC tied our hands at every turn. I just felt useless."

She hasn't changed. She is still warm and kind. As she and the other nurses check me in and prep me, they treat me like a real person, laughing and chatting through the ritual. As I lie there waiting for the surgeon, I watch the TV monitor at my head. I think I can watch the procedure, just like on *House.* The next thing I know, I am waking up in recovery. It is all over and I get a treat: real apple juice and a turkey sandwich. After two days without food, that is fabulous. Also fabulous is the surgeon's news that there is no malignancy and everything is fine.

There is another treat. My ADC *guardians* don't cuff or shackle me on the trip back. It is a demonstration of trust that I deeply appreciate.

Back at the prison, I discover how tired I am. I take a little nap and wake up three hours later. I eat the tray of food they send me and take another nap. At ten o'clock, I wake up, brush my teeth, and am out for the night. It has been a long three days.

For anyone out there dreading a colonoscopy, let me tell you, there's nothing to it, especially if you don't have two days of prep, don't have a Shake, don't have the yucky liquid prison diet, and don't have to go to the hospital with cuffs and shackles. There's always a bright side. I'm actually glad that the prison approved the procedure for me and that the results were clear. I'm healthy and glad to be alive, whether I'm . . . *inside or out.*

Chapter 31

Kitchen Toys

October 2006. I love to cook and I really miss it *inside*. I miss my kitchen toys and the ballet my husband and I did while we were creating our culinary masterpieces. I miss the ingredients we took for granted, the delicious smells, and the tastes.

Cooking in prison is a whole other world. No creative ingredients, utensils, toys, or even a community microwave. Cooking anything is a huge effort and I am not terribly motivated. I have a special hypoglycemic diet and I eat all my meals in the cafeteria. Whereas I used to adore food and lived to eat, in prison I eat to live. Big difference.

Suddenly for the first time in several years, I have a roommate who can really cook. Melanie actually worked as a pastry chef at a local restaurant. She also has the funds to buy the very expensive, occasional treats we can purchase from a charity sale at 100% mark up. All this stimulates her imagination and creativity and the results are marvelous.

Recently, we were allowed to buy rice. Doesn't sound too exciting, does it? Rice-a-Roni, at that. We are rarely served rice and when we are, it is gummy and yucky, so this is a dream come true — until we inspect the box. Instead of instant just-add-water rice, this requires a stove or microwave, neither of which is available here. So, what to do?

Mel isn't daunted for a second. She immediately gets to work boiling water — in our *wastebasket*. Using both of our stingers submerged in about four inches of water, she boils away. Next, she scavenges a plastic bag that our sack lunches come in, those horrid *bag-nasties*. She pours in the rice and loosely measures out the requisite cups of water, mixes it, and ties up the bag. Then she carefully lowers it into the wastebasket of boiling water. She doesn't want the fragile bag to touch the stingers as they might melt the bag, so she decides to use our small plastic mirror to divide the *"bag pot"* from the *"stinger stove."*

The mirror is an interesting kitchen toy for us. We managed to peel off all the foil so all that's left is a three by five inch sheet of clear, hard plastic that we use for cutting everything from rare fruit to bread. It actually works perfectly as a divider to keep the bag intact.

While the rice is cooking, Mel mixes the flavor packet with our butter substitute, mayonnaise. She also adds a few touches of her own from our pathetic supplies and it is fun to watch her work. She loves the cooking process and even in here, with so little, she is having fun and enjoying the creativity.

Twenty minutes later, the rice is done. Mel uses a push-pin to poke holes in the bag and create the perfect strainer. Then she carefully unties the bag, pours the rice into one of our tiny bowls, and carefully mixes in the sauce. Finally, she pronounces it ready to serve and presents it to me as if we are at Buckingham Palace. It is delicious. After our steady diet of bland, very bland, and extra bland, it is heavenly to taste something so different. I'm a big fan of rice anyway so this is a culinary delight for my deprived taste buds.

Mel is somewhat satisfied. She keeps finding little flaws until I burst out laughing and tell her to STOP! After all, she cooked this in a wastebasket! How many cooks could produce such a lovely meal using two stingers, a plastic bag, and a wastebasket? She looks a little sheepish and I coax a smile. She knows it's pretty amazing.

Rice-a-Roni never tasted so good. That's one of the miracles of prison, the ability to be grateful for small, simple pleasures. It's something I never want to lose when I leave here. A grateful heart makes life so much richer and more delicious . . . *inside or out.*

Chapter 32

Compliments

October 2006. Prison is not a place for compliments. I'm not sure why because a system that constantly criticizes and berates creates a person with low self-esteem and high anger. I often wonder how the officers are trained. I know that giving compliments is definitely not part of the curriculum.

Sadly, many inmates don't know how to compliment either. They almost uniformly enter prison with their self-esteem in the gutter. The only thing they're any good at is criticizing and judging. It's their life experience on their path to prison. They face drunken parents and drug-crazed boyfriends before they make it to angry cops, indifferent *public pretenders* (as the inmates call them) and not so indifferent judges. A compliment in prison is a rarity, priceless as a raisin would be if it suddenly appeared in our weekly bowl of corn flakes.

Recently, I received a most unexpected and treasured compliment from Mrs. K., our librarian. Mrs. K. is not a typical prison employee. You can tell that by the look of the library. It is the only place on the yard with green plants, colorful posters, and a purple stuffed bunny to hug. It is bright, cheery, and welcoming. She loves to read aloud and she often reads to her library aides. Occasionally I am privileged to be included. She knows how much I love it and I am a most appreciative audience.

Not everyone likes Mrs. K. Because Santa Cruz is a "medium" yard, there is more security and inmates move by the master pass method. On "minimum" yards, inmates can walk into the library whenever they like, but on Santa Cruz inmates are only allowed to visit one day a week for about twenty minutes and must be on the master list. It's the rule, but it causes grumbling and Mrs. K is the scapegoat.

I like Mrs. K. and appreciate what she has created in the library. It is a little haven in the harshness and I look forward to my weekly visit. We often chat about her three dogs, one rabbit, and a parrot that all live like pashas with treats, toys, food, and for the dogs, almost as many sweaters as Bill Cosby. I miss animals and love her stories about the hilarious antics of Mickey, Minnie and Jade.

Last week Mrs. K. sent for me. I think it is to discuss the cancer awareness corner she is creating for Breast Cancer Awareness Month, but I am wrong. She takes me aside and says she feels compelled to tell me that I have been on her heart recently during this month of cancer awareness. As she speaks, I try to keep the startled look off my face.

"I'll never forget when you got here," she said. "You were so sick and you had so many problems with Medical. You know, cancer outside is bad, but having cancer in here is awful. And you just never gave up. You lost your hair and wore that little beanie that you hated. Some days you even left it off and made no apologies. *This is who I am*, you seemed to say, and you just kept going."

Her big blue eyes fill with tears as do mine.

"People outside talk about heroes, but I think you're a hero in here. You've worked so hard to help people. I don't think these girls know all you've done and I just wanted to tell you I know. You've never given up. I just see you everywhere busy, trying to make a difference and you have. You're a hero."

By now, visibly shaken, big tears roll down my cheeks. Between the tears, I manage a flimsy response.

"Oh, Mrs. K., you have no idea of the gift you have given me. It's simply priceless. If I could only hug you, I would." Of course, hugs are not allowed at Perryville.

There are no words to express the depth of emotions her words of kindness brought forth in me. They were like rain on a parched garden and, like a drooping flower, I soaked them up. If I could have recorded it, I would have played it over and over. Vanity? Pride? I don't think so. I think it's just the desperation we feel inside, desperation for kindness, compassion, laughter, and a priceless compliment.

The few minutes our conversation took will resonate in me as long as I live. For Mrs. K., it was just a compliment. Personally, it was recognition of me as a human being, hope for my future, faith in humanity, and the love of God reflected through the eyes of a small, sweet librarian. It was a pearl beyond price that I will never forget.

A compliment can change so much with just a few words. Isn't it funny how we tend to discard them or refuse to acknowledge their worth? Do me a favor. After you read this, go out and complement the next few people you meet. It can be as simple as liking a tie or as significant as praise for a job well done.

Practice giving compliments.

Yummy dinner.

I love your shirt.

Aren't you pretty?

You did a great job.

Excellent homework.

The house is so clean.

The garden looks wonderful.

I appreciate you.

Trust me, this powerful force of recognition can make a difference in people's lives . . . *inside or out.*

Chapter 33

Piestewa

July 2007. After five years on Santa Cruz, I am to be moved across Citrus Road to Piestewa, a Level 1 transitional unit for inmates with under two years left to serve on their sentence. It is bittersweet.

I learn on June 18th that I am on the movement list and my heart sinks. Although many inmates feel Piestewa is the Promised Land, it's also a dorm with 260 women rather than a cell with a roommate. I remember the slumber party from hell in Estrella Jail. I never stopped shaking there, so the idea of a dorm evokes very bad memories. I decide I'll go and see everyone in every department to try to stop it.

Programs. Can this be stopped? *Nope!* Delayed? *Doubt it.*

Medical. I have limited duty. Do they take limited duty at Piestewa? *Yes.* What about my meds? Will that stop me? *No.* Can the doctor stop this move? *No.*

Deputy Warden Bailey. Can you stop this move? *Don't you want to go?* I don't know. What's best? *Well, it's best for me and Santa Cruz if you stay, but best for you if you go.*

With these answers, I know it's time to talk to God. It's a one-sided conversation.

"Now look, God." Of course God knows what I want and need, but I spell it out anyway. "You need to delay the move until I'm caught up with all of my paperwork and lesson plans and I've found replacements for all my programs — say a month."

I do ask when I'll move, but ADC will never tell you. "It's a security risk." I might call my friends to plot an escape as I ride across the street. Never mind that I went to the hospital for radiation every day at exactly the same time for six weeks and never remotely thought of escape. That doesn't figure into the equation. It has to be a surprise.

So I wake up everyday for weeks wondering if this is moving day, then go to work. As the weeks pass, even Administration begins to wonder why on earth I haven't moved. Women are moving all around me, but I am still here. I know why. It's God. I have the time to find replacements for my programs and say a proper goodbye to the many people who have been important on my journey.

Gale is happy to take over the *Red Hats* with the enthusiastic help of Natalie and Nancy. They have big plans and I believe it will grow and be even better.

The *Cancer Support Group* is tougher. No one in the group has the passion for it that I have, but then Leah comes along. Only twenty-five years old, she had a lumpectomy while serving time in federal prison. Right before she was transferred to ADC, they found a lump in her other breast, but there was no time to begin treatment. This new opportunity will give her something to do while she waits for Medical to begin her treatment.

Gavel Club is easy. There is a new slate of officers and I have every confidence it will live on and continue to inspire others. I am really proud of that group because I see visible changes in the members.

Life Skills is my pet. Thankfully, Valerie and Tracey jump in, and I know they'll do a great job. I bring all the lesson plans up to date, move the library over to Tracey's yard and reassure the class they are in wonderful hands. I then go to the C.O.IV to ask if Piestewa would be interested in any of my programs. If so, would they like me to bring a box of materials over when I move?

"Good idea," he said. "I'll let you know."

Two days later, I receive a memo with permission to take a box of materials over with me. That is unheard of and I am pleased, thankful, and surprised. I pack one box that overflows into two boxes of priceless teaching materials collected over my years here and I begin the waiting game.

While I wait, I say more goodbyes. I've taught many inmates whose lives touched mine in deeply meaningful ways and I want to wish them well. There are also officers I want to thank for their kindness and courtesy to me and I am glad I take the time because they all seem a bit stunned and genuinely grateful. Several get tears in their eyes, but one stops me cold. When I thank Mr. R., he holds out his hand to shake mine, knowing officers are not supposed to ever touch us. It feels like the most amazing acknowledgement of me as a human being. I take a breath and meet his grasp, then turn and flee to my room where I burst into tears over his generosity of spirit. I am not used to such humanity in prison. He has given me a gift and all I can do is cry.

I also make an appointment to see Ms. Bailey. I tell her I can not imagine what this prison journey would have been like without her leadership and kindness. Without her there would be no Cancer Walk, no Cancer Support Group, no Red Hat Society, no Gavel Club, and no Life Skills. She always said yes to my proposals and her approval gave me purpose. As I speak, I start to cry and then she starts to cry and then we are crying and laughing at the same time. She is a rare combination of compassion and toughness, infinitely practical and full of common sense. She sees inmates as human beings. I will never forget her.

I say my goodbyes and continue to wait, wondering each day if I'll pack up. It gets hotter and hotter until the temperature reaches 117 degrees and I tell God I am ready in case God needs a gentle reminder. Then the C.O.IV tells me they found a Medical hold on my file from 2003 when I was going through radiation. On Thursday it is lifted and on Tuesday I move. It is one month since my conversation with God. I arranged a smooth transition and even celebrated my birthday, definitely a gift from God.

The pack up is another of ADC's wacky systems. At 7:30 in the evening I am told to pack up. I take down my room décor — my bulletin board of pets. Arrange my food items so they won't get smushed. Make sure none of the hygiene leaks (Wish I had zip lock bags). Fold up clothes. Cram all the extra files and books into the legal boxes. At nine o'clock, I'm done and the waiting begins. Ten o'clock. Eleven o'clock. Midnight. At one o'clock in the morning, the grave-yard shift summons me.

My roommate, Darcy, and I load all my worldly goods onto a cart and schlep it out to the picnic area where we unload it. There in pitch darkness, the officer does inventory using a very small flashlight she bought herself because ADC doesn't provide one. It takes ninety minutes. Then Darcy and I reload the cart and push it up to the yard office. It is 2:30 in the morning and the prison yard is at rest, calm, cool, and beautifully quiet. It is my first time out after 8:30 in the evening since 2003. Even with Darcy beside me, I feel completely alone, yet completely full of the Universe, one with the sky and the trees and all the sleeping women behind the steel doors. It is a silence I can feel, full of the presence of the Infinite.

I have to be up at 4:30 so I make no effort to sleep. I lie on my bunk in the stillness and remember the last five years. At 4:30, I shake off my memories and go to find Valerie who is normally running the track at that time. It is the moment we've been dreading. Finding someone here with her gentle sensitivity, intelligence, and *joie de vivre* (after all, she is French), was a tremendous blessing. I will always treasure her friendship and kindness to me over the past year. I will miss her greatly.

Shower, breakfast, and more waiting. Usually the van comes at 7:30, but not this day. It is 9:15 before I am finally called for the next part of my prison journey. More loading — into the van, cross the street, out of the van, into the cafeteria. It's 110 degrees and I feel like I have an oven strapped to my back. In the cafeteria, suddenly the world is cool; it's air conditioning. It feels **heavenly**. In the coolness everything is re-inventoried by another C.O.II. (Job security.) I don't mind; I'm soaking in the A.C. At last it's done and I load the cart one last time to go to the dorm. (Ominous background music plays.)

The dorm is clean and quiet and very cool. My space is tiny. I have the lower bunk in an area about five foot by seven foot. It holds the bed, cupboard, and walking space. To change anything, including my mind, I have to step outside. But it's okay. It's air-conditioned and feels very peaceful. There are some women here from Santa Cruz and they come to welcome me, worried I will miss the privacy of my room. Well, of course I do, but not enough to fret.

Sitting on my bunk, I realize just how stressful it is to live in the Arizona heat, trying to keep cool when it's 110 degrees. I begin to notice differences. My hair is fluffy and not stuck to my head. My clothes are dry and smell nice. They smell nice because they were washed and dried in proper machines and not in a wastebasket. Luxury!

There's another civilized perk — microwaves. At Santa Cruz, we cooked Rice-a-Roni in the all-purpose wastebasket with a stinger and, despite Mel's best efforts, the rice was always gummy. At Piestewa, I cook my Rice-a-Roni in the microwave and it is fluffy and delicious. Sure beats a wastebasket/stove.

I was worried about the noise, but that worry is unfounded. During the day and after nine at night, it is very quiet. Just like the real world, *Happy Hour* is between five and six when everyone is back from work and busy sharing the day. Even then it is never the decibel level of Estrella. After five years at Santa Cruz, Piestewa is indeed the Promised Land. There are women here who complain, but there are complainers everywhere, and everywhere they are unhappy. Whether in prison or in a palace, some people just love to complain. Grumbling doesn't feel good to me. I'd rather be grateful and I am so grateful to be in a clean, air conditioned place.

Joseph Stalin said, *"Gratitude is a sickness suffered by dogs."* And we know what he did. On the other hand, Henry Ward Beecher said, *"Gratitude is the fairest blossom which springs from the soul."*

I'll go with that one and have a garden of flowers in my soul, wherever I am . . . *inside or out.*

Chapter 34

Punishment or Correction

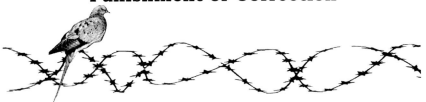

July 2007. Now that I am living in air conditioning again for the first time in many years, I've started to think about the purpose of prison. Is it to punish or to correct? In prison, the staff tells us they are not here to punish us. Our punishment is our separation from society. That is indeed a very big punishment. But why do I feel there is no correction? What does that have to do with air conditioning?

On a day when the temperature has been about 112 degrees for many days, put on your heaviest polyester pants and t-shirt, go out in your garage with a very small fan, and spend the day. Have lunch there, soup (yes, soup) and a balogna sandwich. Sweep, mop and clean, watch TV, read. Try to nap on a plastic cot, eat a lukewarm dinner, spend the night. This is Arizona prison in the summer.

Summer lasts nearly four months, 1440 minutes a day of sheer, unrelenting, blast furnace heat. The small bit of grass on the field chokes and turns brown. The few prized trees are gasping and piti-ful. Looking forlorn, the birds wander into the community showers to drink the stagnant water pooling on the hot concrete. The prairie dogs wisely burrow under ground.

The prison yards on Perryville are very spread out. We walk ev-erywhere, blocks and blocks between buildings. No shade. The ad-ministration offices and classrooms are air-conditioned, but that's it. Evaporative coolers slog away to cool the cells and cafeterias. They work until the temperature hits 90 degrees. After that, the cells become concrete coffins of heat. There is no relief.

They've actually done studies that show evaporative coolers are environmentally inefficient and costly. They use more power and water than air-conditioning, but ADC keeps repairing the thirty year old coolers, knowing nobody cares about inmates and their health. In Arizona, it is a health issue. There is more heat exhaustion than I can count, and one summer, when the temperature had been 117 degrees for days, there were nineteen heat related seizures in one morning. It all ends up costing money in Medical attention. One way or another, the tax payer pays.

My first summer at Perryville was horrific. The previous director had retired the year before, leaving a final gift to the inmates. He had all the inmates' fans removed. In Arizona, that would be cruel under normal conditions, but I was going through radiation and my chest was burned, raw, and bleeding. I'd had such a severe reaction that the radiologist called a two week hiatus so I'd heal a bit.

Christine, my partner in cancer treatment, had worse blisters than I did. We were both suffering from the searing pain exacerbated by the heat. Christine's father actually called the prison, offering to buy a couple of fans for Medical use as a humanitarian gesture. Request denied.

In the middle of June, when Gina died, the heat added to her misery. Finally, Gina's death opened some eyes and fans were approved once more. They push the scorching air around and keep us tepid rather than boiling.

The five summers I spent on Santa Cruz before moving to Piestewa were torture. Each year, I passed out from the heat. Once, an officer found me unconscious on the floor of my room. Twice, I collapsed on the yard on the searing concrete, and once I was sweeping and I just fell out over the threshold. Besides the heat, the pill I take to keep the cancer at bay causes hot flashes as a side effect. Sitting in a concrete coffin of heat with hot flashes is a different kind of torture.

Let's get back to your garage. What can you do in your stifling garage to relieve the heat? You can't go to the fridge for an ice cold coke. You can buy a ten-pound bag of ice for $2.24, about a day's salary if you are lucky enough to make 30¢ an hour. For another $1.35, you can buy a very small, thin Styrofoam cooler to keep the ice in. The ice melts in a few hours, but meanwhile, you can have ice cold water, and that is a luxury. You can also wet down your shirt and head. That helps. You can wear a wet washcloth around your neck. You can fill an old hair spray bottle with water and spray yourself continuously, sort of like the misters at an outdoor café. That's pretty much it. Even the showers are scalding. Maintenance refuses to go to the trouble of turning the hot water off in the summer. No relief there, no relief anywhere.

My friend Krissy was in R&A the summer the water and power went off. The entire yard was locked down for three days. No water, no showers, no flushing, no evaporative coolers in the six foot by eleven foot concrete coffin. Staff delivered inmate meals with one eight-ounce Styrofoam cup of water that was gratefully gulped. Krissy tried to stay as still as possible, but she and her bunkie poured sweat, constantly using their washcloths to wipe the sweat off. She said she will never forget the feeling of desperation, locked in that suffocating cell, or the rancid stink of that washcloth.

There are as many opinions about the purpose of prisons as there are inmates in America. Punishment is much higher on the list than rehabilitation and America's prisons are designed to punish. Many people think that inmates don't deserve more than two or three cups of water a day and a rancid washcloth. What does that teach? It certainly doesn't teach a person to be kind or considerate. It does, however, teach inmates that they are worthless, disposable human beings.

Before prison, I was a confident woman. Prison ate away at my confidence. I was always afraid and wondered what had happened to my confidence? I realized then just how much prison had affected me. It is a daily Chinese water torture of denigration, and if I was affected so dramatically, imagine what it does to others lacking confidence.

In the end, it boils down to humanity. Is this who we really are? Are we a nation that prefers to punish in such dehumanizing ways? Are we really teaching people a lesson? What we are doing is treating people so badly that they become bitter, angry, and mean, completely unprepared for a life of civility and respect.

I learned other things in prison. I learned that everyone wants love, but many in prison have never had it, from parents, friends, or partners. Prison is full of horror stories, but the worst was about the girl on my yard whose name I never knew, and she had a nickname too awful to repeat. She had been abused by all the men in her family and repeatedly raped by her father. At twelve, she became pregnant with her father's child and at thirteen, gave birth to her son who was also her brother. I believe she had Attention Deficit Disorder because she was never still, always acting out, and frequently in trouble. She was desperate for love and attention, but had no idea how to get it. Of course, she was in prison. The abusive men were free.

I also learned that all the great thinkers were right; Jesus, Buddha, John Lennon, and Jackie DeShannon *(Put a Little Love in Your Heart)* were right. All we need is love. Of course, that's simplistic and we have made it complicated. We have become a nation of fear and anger. We'd rather flex our muscles than flex our hearts. Love seems to always have conditions.

I could make this really long, detailing what we need to do, but we all know; we're just not doing it. Be kind, be considerate, be respectful, stop judging. Open our hearts. Think about others first. Ask yourself, "Is this who I am as a human being?" Don't you dare yawn. You know it's true and you know it works . . . *inside and out.*

Chapter 35

Judgment

September 2007. There are 260 women at Piestewa. Many share the experience of abuse, others are addicts. Most have experienced the horrors of Estrella Jail. We've all been judged by the courts and society. There is a broad common bond of sorrow, pain, and grief, and yet we can not get along. Sometimes, the race to judgment and the lack of compassion take my breath away.

I first notice it at Estrella where everyone is the same, all dressed in those hideous black and white stripes, sticky and sweaty in the heat. The conditions are hostile; the guards are demeaning; the atmosphere is dark and heavy. The lines of division are obvious. It is "them" vs. "us". We are all sisters, sharing a common grief, but we can't even get that right. We are a dysfunctional family, pathetic lost souls with little idea how to come together in compassion.

We've all been in court, listening to prosecutors tell their version of the truth. They paint the defendants with a broad brush of darkness while the defense brings in their brush of light. Somewhere in the middle is the truth, a human being encompassing both dark and light, neither as dastardly nor as pure as painted in court.

Nevertheless, knowing this, the Judge picks up his brush and adds to the canvas of despair. We are judged and no one likes it. You have to stand there and keep your mouth shut, even when it is unfair and unbalanced; even when you lose your children, your home, your freedom. You are judged and you hate it.

That same day, upon return to the jail, you pick up where the judge left off. Addicts judge thieves who judge prostitutes. They all judge child abusers who are considered the lowest of the low in prison. It's a twisted pride of "my crimes are not as bad as yours." But we're all here for a crime, all judged by society and staff. What is it about human nature that takes such glee in judging?

When I left the jail and got to the prison yard, I found the judging was here too, but I could go to my room and escape it. Most of the chatter went on in the smoking section over card games, and I wasn't a part of that. The room was small, but it was a sanctuary that kept the negativity at bay.

Suddenly I am moved to Piestewa where I am surrounded by women in a dorm where the neighbors are only two feet away. There is simply no escape. We are stacked up like boxes on a shelf and we hear everything. One day, I was washing my hands in the bathroom when an argument started between two women. It was loud but brief, ending sharply when one called the other a fucking whore. I expected there to be blows, but the one being attacked turned quickly and walked away. She has five weeks left on her sentence and doesn't want to do anything to jeopardize that.

That name calling is common here. I heard it yelled across the room in the dining hall one morning. Sometimes I learn what triggers it; sometimes I don't. It's never earth shattering or even deserved. It's a quick judgment, a typical knee-jerk reaction. Yesterday I was yelled at over laundry. The washer was done. I waited awhile for the person to come take out their clothes. I followed protocol. I announced to the dorm, "Washer's done." No one came, so finally I put the clothes in the dryer.

Much later, an angry woman stood by my bed, furious that I had touched her clothes. I apologized profusely and said that I'd just done what I'd want someone to do for me. I assured her that *my hands were very clean.* She went away grumbling, but others have come to blows over the same situation. FYI, we aren't talking about Chanel here; these were ADC uniforms. Why so touchy? When I think about this group of women with similar pain and despair who cannot get along, how in the world can we expect the Sunnis and Shias to agree, or the Palestinians and Israelis? Two of our officers came to blows in the parking lot recently before cooler heads prevailed. What could be so important? Usually in a few weeks they can't even remember what the big deal was. We should apply the 10/10/10 rule I read about in Oprah. Will this matter in 10 minutes, 10 weeks, or 10 years? Usually the answer is a resounding NO.

I act like I'm a perfect observer when nothing could be further from the truth. I am right there with the best of them, all the while reading books on the *Power of Positive Thinking*. I know all the old adages: *Like begets like; What goes around comes around; Judge not least you be judged.* I know it and yet I judge, particularly when I'm feeling insecure and alone. I feel very alone, in the midst of 259 women.

Have you ever caught yourself judging? Where does it come from? With me, it comes from my father. I was never enough for him. Never smart enough, pretty enough, thin enough, careful enough. Everyone in our society has been judged by someone else and found *not enough.* And we don't like it. So why do we keep doing it? Why is our culture based on this system of competition and judging? How can we stop the cycle?

The funny thing is I am judging the negativity by being negative. I am feeding the beast with the fuel of my criticism, just adding to the despair. As I watch my words unfold, I realize that's just plain NUTS.

I feel so sad when people don't look into my heart to see how much I care. Yet by judging others, I'm refusing to look into their hearts. What is the drive behind their behavior, their anger, their kindness, or their cruelty? That is always my challenge and my opportunity. Prison is the perfect place to practice, a sort of crash-course in Compassion 101. I want to graduate before release. After all, seeing into the hearts of others is a priceless ability, one we can all use . . . *inside and out.*

Chapter 36

Food Visits

November 2007. The women are giddy. Their excitement rises like clouds of cheap hair spray over the dorm. It is one of our quarterly food visits and all that it implies. Four times a year, family and friends are allowed to visit, bringing all the food their inmate can consume in four hours. We are not allowed to share it with other inmates or bring the leftovers back to the ladies who don't get visits. Essentially, it is an orgy of eating, but no sharing.

There are, of course, reams of rules. Everything must be packed in clear plastic bags and Tupperware. Real plastic forks and spoons instead of orange plastic sporks. No plastic knives, no foil, no fruit. That is my biggest disappointment. No fruit. I miss fruit desperately and was eager for peaches from Carolyn's tree. No peaches, no oatmeal raisin cookies, no blueberry pound cake, no strawberry cheesecake. I wonder why.

My friends explain. A clever cook can soak the fruit in alcohol for their alcoholic inmate friends. Fruit is practically non-existent in prison because the officials fear inmates will make hooch, a nasty mixture of fermented fruit mixed with stale bread and sugar. I saw and smelled it once at Estrella Jail, but the thought of actually drinking it was terrifying. The smell was vile, the consistency was nasty, and it was full of tiny bugs floating around. Not exactly a bartender's delight.

There is no doubt there are some serious addicts in prison, but there are also serious health issues like diabetes, cancer, and heart disease. ADC never considers being proactive by serving more fresh fruit or at least selling us real fruit juice from the store like they do at the federal prisons. Staff is sick of me lobbying for V-8 juice. I am grateful to be hypoglycemic. Instead of cake or cookies, I get fruit at most meals, usually an orange, but sometimes an apple if I am lucky. Too often, it is canned pears or applesauce.

Diane and Carolyn, my cherished friends, eagerly stumble through the minefield of rules and regulations to prepare the picnic of my dreams. Most inmates want KFC, pizza, or other fast food. Some want steak, as we are very meat deprived. I want tomatoes and a vegetarian feast. They come loaded with a clear plastic box, filled with jewels of vegetables — tomatoes, avocados, jicama, and zucchini. Heaven. There is a bag of fresh salad greens and two kinds of dressing, but I want to savor everything separately with nothing to change the taste. There is also a plate of vegetable side dishes from Boston Market: garlic spinach, green beans, squash, and mashed, sweet potatoes. And finally, yogurt for dessert. The Captain has somehow gotten fruit yogurt approved if it is in the original, sealed store container. I ask for peach and berry.

I start very slowly with the tomatoes and proceed to relish every perfect bite. The emotions connected to that simple, healthy, delicious food bring tears to my eyes. I cry from gratitude and delight. It has been so long. The one-third cup of vegetables we get at dinner is usually over–cooked. Mostly, it is over-cooked carrots, but sometimes we get lucky and have over-cooked broccoli. At lunch, it's beans. Couple that with a half cup of iceberg lettuce drowned in terrible dressing and you can see why the food visit is so wonderful.

I stagger back to the dorm, stuffed to the brim with barely room to breathe, giddy with the joy of my opulent meal. Besides the food, the company was glorious. Prison conversations tend to center around legal issues: crimes, cases, judgments, jail time, guards, and other inmates. Very negative. My food visit, on the other hand, was centered on real conversation. We talked about food, movies, fashion, politics, and travel, laughing between bites. It was a banquet of gourmet food and gourmet conversation.

Prison and food visits raise my appreciation of all the slow things that people take for granted in the outside world. Cell phones are fast. Blackberries are fast. E-mail is fast. Traffic is fast. Sound bytes are fast. Even food is fast. No time for gratitude. *Hurry, hurry, hurry!*

I have learned to slow down. Nothing is that important. Think about the wonder of slow things: slow hugs, slow dancing, slow summer days at the lake, slow winter nights in front of the fire, slow walks with someone you love, and family dinners, eaten slowly. That's what inmates think about in prison. I know I sound preachy, but please, slow down and be grateful. Life can change in a heartbeat and then it's too late. Slow and grateful are good things . . . *inside and out.*

Chapter 37

This Too Shall Pass

May 2008. I'll never forget the day a young student of mine approached me with downcast eyes. She seemed embarrassed. "Can I ask you a question?"

"Sure," I said, "I love questions."

She stammered a bit before blurting out a caveat, "Please don't be mad at me and take this wrong."

I promised I wouldn't.

Finally she took a deep breath and mumbled, "You've gone through so much here. At your age, how do you keep going?"

"Well," I laughed, "What are the alternatives?"

I know about the alternatives. I am surrounded by all kinds of alternatives. They call them addictions. In prison (and out) there are drugs and alcohol and pain meds. There is gambling, there is suicide. Honestly, none of those seems very attractive. Intuitively I know that addiction is only a temporary fix. Eventually, I have to come back to the world and its problems.

Then there was that other part of the question. . .at your age.

"How old are you?" I asked.

"Twenty-eight," she said.

"Well," I asked, "how old is old to you?"

"I guess forty."

"And if you were forty, what would you consider old?"

"I guess fifty-five."

"Okay, what if you were fifty-five, what would be old?"

"I guess, sixty-five or seventy."

"I read somewhere that we think old is fifteen years older than we are. Based on what you've said, that would be right. No wonder I seem ancient to you."

On my fifteenth birthday, I was feeling very cool, with the arrogance of a teenager. My mother burst my bubble when she said,

"Well, Sue Ellen, you're half way to thirty now."

That seemed ancient. Didn't Bob Dylan say "Never trust anyone over thirty?" I couldn't be halfway! Suddenly, in the blink of an eye, I was thirty (and Bob Dylan was thirty four) and it wasn't so bad. As a matter of fact, my thirties were pretty good. And just as suddenly, I was forty. Forty sounded ancient, but it wasn't. The forties were pretty good too. Then came fifty and I knew that was going to be really bad, but it wasn't. The fifties were fine too, except for the breast cancer and the trip to prison. And now I'm in my sixties. The sixties aren't bad either. I feel great and work out every morning. I have more energy than many of the young women I know here. They drag around, whining and complaining, and gossiping a lot. All that will drain your energy quite effectively.

Whining, complaining, crying, blaming: definitely the alternatives when things fall apart. Now tears I understand. I've cried an ocean here. It's such a sad place. But thankfully, I never cry for very long. It's exhausting and it's boring. I don't like to be exhausted or bored. So I keep going. To quote Woody Allen, "Eighty percent of success is showing up." In prison, many people don't even do that. They have an excuse for everything, an issue that takes them to the smoking section and the card table. Any issue will do. They have no history of making a commitment and sticking with it.

I remember one very hard day in prison. David and I were told that our early release date had been denied. Everything had finally been approved and we were looking forward to the day when we would be together again. Then, ironically on Friday the 13th, we were given the bad news. My heart stopped for a beat. I was stunned. Why? WHY? No one knew. Not my counselor or his boss or anyone in authority. No one at David's yard knew either. They were stunned too. We were model inmates. They'd never seen this happen before. As we found out later, the whys would fill another chapter.

Meanwhile, the next day I had a class to teach. I told the students what had happened and they wanted to know why I hadn't cancelled class. Because that's not an excuse for cancelling anything. When you get bad news, your world stops for an instant; you start it back up and keep on going. The other choices lead to addiction and that welcomed numbness, but that doesn't help. What helps is getting up again.

I will never forget my thirtieth birthday. It was the beginning of the long July 4th weekend. My boss called me into his office late Thursday afternoon to tell me there were budget cuts. The department was being reorganized and there were layoffs. I was *laid-off.* That is a politically correct term for fired.

Numbly, I went home to call my boyfriend. We were due to go away for the long holiday weekend and I definitely needed a compassionate shoulder to lean on. Only it wasn't forthcoming. He took this golden opportunity to tell me he needed some *space.* Have you ever heard that one? On top of being fired, he was breaking up with me. And to top that off, **I was thirty.** I knew it could not get worse.

I contemplated suicide. I wanted to die but I didn't want to hurt myself. If I drove into a tree, I might be paralyzed. Pills could make me sick. Slashed wrists; too gory. Instead, I spent three days floating around the pool at my apartment feeling monumentally sorry for myself. I am ashamed to say the pity party didn't last three days; it lasted three years. I got another job and had plenty of dates, but I just couldn't get over that terrible weekend. I was pathetic, self-absorbed, and very poor company.

I'm also ashamed to say it took me years to discover there is a better way. What I should have done that long, lonely, miserable weekend was gotten in the car and gone straight to St. Vincent de Paul or one of the Food Banks to volunteer. The best medicine is doing something for someone else to get the pain out of your mind. It may not take the nausea away. Sure, the pain is still there. However, every occupied moment creates a little distraction that helps, a little distance from the pain. The more you work, the more distance there is, and then suddenly you realize that the pain has faded. First it's just for a moment, but then it's longer and longer until you don't remember the jerk at all. *This too shall pass.* Those four little words are definitely part of life's great secrets.

So back to the original question, "How do I keep going at my age?" Because I know the alternatives and I don't like them. I prefer to think *this too shall pass.* I know it's true. At my age, a lot has passed. The incidents pass and the emotions pass. Can you remember that terrible fight you had with your husband, sister, mother, friend, child? It seemed so important at the time. You didn't speak for days and now you can't remember what it was about. *This too shall pass.* Imagine the person who is still carrying the fight around. Their baggage must weigh a ton. Lighten your load. Forgive and forget, because I promise the dramas add up and the bags get heavier. *This too shall pass.* It's a great mantra to have . . . *inside or out.*

"Do all the good you can, in all the places you can, at all the times you can, to all the people you can, as long as you ever can."

John Wesley (1703-1792)

Chapter 38

The Elephant in the Room

November 2007. One of the greatest unknowns about prison and certainly one of the most frightening is the strip search. I wasn't going to write about it, but then I realized it's the elephant in the room and cannot be ignored.

I had my first strip search upon entering Estrella Jail when I changed from my street clothes to the infamous black and white stripes chosen to add extra humiliation to the whole jail experience. I was in a total daze. We had flown from New Jersey the day before and I'd been up for about thirty hours. I'd been crammed into a twelve foot by twelve foot holding tank with about thirty-six other women. I'd been given a tiny bit of unidentifiable food, but I was too nauseated to eat. I'd just had my sixth session of chemotherapy recently and I was definitely feeling the poison.

Now a grumpy officer was telling me to strip for her and numbly I complied. Carefully, I folded my black gabardine slacks and pink knit sweater. (When would I ever see them again?) Then I learned there is a proper routine for a strip search. Starting at the top, first you open your mouth widely so she can see that you aren't hiding drugs. Then, you lean forward and show behind your ears after which you flip your hair to show nothing is hiding there. Most of the women have very long hair, but I'd lost mine to chemo. When she automatically told me to flip my hair, I must have looked rather sad because, despite her gruffness, she did look a bit sheepish.

Next, I had to spread my toes and show her the bottoms of my feet. Finally, she told me to squat and cough three times and, while I was bent over, I was told to spread the cheeks of my derriere. She didn't call it that though. I suppose this is the ultimate humiliation, especially for a woman of my age and dignity.

I tried to take my mind to another place. I haven't always been old and dignified. Back in the dark ages, as a student at the University of Texas, I lived in a dorm, sharing a bathroom with three other young women of nice, modest families. After a few weeks, we tossed our modesty out of the window. There were times when all of us would be in the bathroom at once — one brushing her teeth, one using the toilet as a chair, one in the tub, and one just hanging out, sharing gossip, beauty tips, or class notes.

Sylvia was usually the one in the tub. I remember her surrounded by bubbles with her strawberry blonde hair piled high on her head, sparkling blue eyes, creamy white skin, and always her pearls. She loved those pearls. They were a graduation gift from her grandmother who told her to wear them often so the natural oil from her skin would add luster to the pearls. Our nakedness didn't bother us then. Why should it bother me now?

I suppose it is the vulnerability. I always feel so vulnerable in my nakedness, and if the officer is hostile it makes it worse. It must be a bit like rape. Rape is the ultimate degradation for any woman, when she feels completely and utterly helpless and vulnerable. I've never been raped, but many of the women in prison have. They talk about it casually to gloss over the pain, but I wondered if the strip search brings back that pain, the fear, and the helplessness.

All the inmates who work off the yard are stripped every day, just in case they are trying to smuggle in a pair of scissors from the print shop or a needle from the garment factory. Since I don't work off-site, I am spared that. The strip is bad enough, but the strip shack is freezing in the winter and broiling in the summer, just to add injury to insult.

I did have to strip every day when I was going to radiation. Radiation is bad enough, but the strip just adds to the agony. Inmates are also stripped after every visit in case some visitor has tried to smuggle in God knows what — usually drugs, but since Perryville is a woman's prison, lip-gloss and perfume samples are more likely.

There are some women here who try to avoid strips at all costs. Bev is sixty-four years old, very fragile and dignified. She hasn't seen her family in years because she hates to be stripped. She is an extreme case. On the other hand, some women never get visits. They would be thankful for a post-visit strip.

I am grateful for my visits and try to zip through the strip as quickly as possible. After every visit, four inmates at a time go into a classroom and stand between long tables that are positioned at tall angles to create dividers and a semblance of privacy. The officers can see the inmates; the other inmates can't see each other. I know the drill. Strip off your clothes, place on the chair, and wait for the C.O. Start at the top . . . aahh, flip, squat, cough, spread, dress, done.

You know what I hate? I hate that since my mastectomy, I only have one breast and I stand there naked with my lopsided chest on view, feeling vulnerable. I decide to combat the feeling and I stand up, completely straight and proud. I know I always have a choice and I chose to stand straight, lopsided or not.

Life is about choices. I made choices that took me to prison and I make choices every day while I am here, choices to maintain my sanity, my dignity, my humanity. It is not easy. Some days I feel lonely, some days I am afraid, some days I cry. But, every day I make the choice to stand up straight and walk tall. It's good to remember we all have a choice . . . *inside and out.*

Chapter 39

Sustenance

January 2008. Inmates are sustained by three hots and a cot, and given the minimum to feed, clothe, and house them. The idea is that one should never be comfortable in prison. And yet, some are comfortable here. Some women feel safer here than outside. They are free from the angry fists of a hateful husband or the seductive temptations of the friendly drug dealer.

Mabel was a tiny woman in her fifties with a blank look, the result of too much medication. Mabel wasn't sure where she was half of the time. Once during the summer, she told me that the unbearable heat reminded her of her home in Phoenix. She could only work as a pod porter cleaning showers because she couldn't pass the mandatory 8th grade proficiency test. The younger women teased her and were often cruel to her. She was always glad to see me because I spoke kindly to her and would help her with the trash if I saw her. She generally tried to carry the huge trash barrels alone and they were almost bigger than she was.

One day Mabel is released and I say a silent prayer for her safety. She's *killed her number* which means she's served her whole sentence because she had nowhere to go. If you kill your number, ADC has no control over you when you are releaased. No parole, no probation, no halfway house. Mabel leaves with fifty dollars and complete freedom. But where does a fifty – something woman with no education and a mental disorder go with fifty dollars, dressed in cast-off prison blues?

The courts locked her up to punish her. I never knew her crime. She cleaned showers and raked rocks while Medical drugged her up to keep her calm. No programs or education are available for an inmate like her. She did her time and she left, but there is no place for her to go except a shelter and how does she do that? She has no idea where one is and how to get there. When you kill your number,

ADC's not much interested in where you go and fifty dollars sure won't take you far.

One day about eight months later I see Mabel again. She is back and happy to see a familiar face. She tells me she is glad to be back. She'd been sleeping under hedges in a park and was cold and hungry. At least in prison, her body is sustained.

There are too many women like Mabel here. Because Congress has cut aid to mental illness over the years, nearly one-fourth of all women inmates are on some kind of psych meds. Women with mental illness are easy prey for men who can get them to sell their drugs or their bodies and then take the rap for them. They are mostly poor and can't afford Medical help. In most cases, they have no clue where to get help or what to ask for. They drop out of school because they can't keep up. Often their families abuse them and treat them like slaves.

I met Martha at Estrella Jail when she asked me if I could teach her to read. Martha was a forty-eight year old woman whose family had locked her in a closet during most of her childhood. When she was older and beaten into submission, they finally let her out to use as a babysitter/maid/cook to take care of the house and the younger children. No school allowed for Martha. She was a quiet, gentle soul with a perpetually frightened look. The constant noise of the dorm was horribly stressful and she was on meds for severe depression. I empathized with her. When the younger girls screamed, we shook together. And there was a lot of screaming.

The guards at the jail said I was wasting my time trying to teach Martha to read, but she soaked up my help, desperate to learn and pitifully grateful for my attention. She cried when I was transferred to Perryville.

Six months later, I hear my name called across the yard and there is Martha. Finally sentenced, she is here, very happy to see me and show off to her teacher. Without any help after I left, she kept my notes and laboriously stumbled through her Bible, teaching herself more and more each day, an amazing accomplishment. Once here, she managed to pass the eighth grade proficiency test before her release. Finally released, where did she go? Where does a fifty-five year old woman go with an eighth grade education, fifty dollars, and a hunger to learn?

Simone is a darling twenty-five year old who behaves like a six week old puppy, desperate for attention and love, a non-stop movement machine. Simone has ADD and is bi-polar. She takes lots of meds, but they don't keep her quiet. Her story of rape and abuse by family members is common in prison. Here she is safe from the men but not from herself. As a product of her past, she is a walking-talking disaster. In about three weeks, she got three tickets. Desperate for attention, that is one way to get it. My roommate says if you are nice to her, she thinks it is sexual. She has no idea how to just have a friend.

Some people would judge Simone harshly as a trouble-maker, but how can any of us know how we would be if we'd had her life? To be so abused and raped by your own family, I cannot begin to imagine. I'm amazed she acts like a love-starved puppy and not a hate-filled murderer. I've looked in her eyes and seen her desperate need to be loved.

I cannot judge Mabel, Maria, or Simone. Before prison, I would have seen only their record and behavior and just written them off like so much rubbish. Then, like them, I was written off. I came to prison where I've gotten to know these women. I hear their stories and look into their eyes. I see their sorrow and their desperate longing. Oh, they cover up their emotions with smart mouths, arrogance, and anger, but they can't cover up the longing, longing for their children, their families, their very selves.

I call my prison journey a gift. Before prison, my life was based on other people's opinions. Did I wear the right clothes, drive the right car, have the right job, live in the right house? That's what sustained my superficial self. Now after prison, who cares?

What sustains me now? The desire to serve these forgotten women and to make a difference in their lives. I've been blessed with a talent to teach and an education to share. I am blessed to be allowed to create and teach *Life Skills* at the prison. My goal is to inspire them to think about themselves in new ways and see new possibilities for their future, to fill the empty space of longing with a new awareness of themselves. There are so many lives to touch and I am thankful for the opportunity. My classes sustain my spirit along with my dream to continue this vision upon release. Yes, I plan to go back to prison, only this time as a volunteer, dressed in any color but orange. There are many Mabels, Marias, and Simones all waiting for a helping hand . . . *inside and out.*

Chapter 40

Field Trip

December 2008. It is 6 o'clock on the Tuesday before Thanksgiving. I look up from my book to see a sergeant standing in my cube holding a blue duffle bag. "Pack up, Allen. You're moving." My eyebrows rise and my heart sinks. After a year and a half on Piestewa, I know there is no place to go but down or out, and I know I'm not getting out. Where on earth am I going?

Suddenly my small space is filled with friends and students, all as dismayed as I am. Trying not to panic, I rush up to the Administration office to see the C.O.IV. Only hours before, she told me I wasn't going anywhere. On the same day, the Medical provider had also said I would not be moved. Why had I asked? Because the day before, one of my friends had been unexpectedly moved to Santa Maria. That was unsettling.

We had heard that ADC had decided to move inmates considered chronic care and cancer survivors are chronic care. However, at my stage as a seven year survivor, it means I only get a blood test every six months. I take no special meds and get no special treatment. So where am I going and why? The C.O.IV has no clue and is embarrassed. She promises to e-mail the deputy warden, but once a move is ordered, it is like a boulder rushing down a mountain. There is no stopping it.

I think I'll go to Santa Maria with Nikki. *Ok, I can handle that. I know people at Maria. It will be all right.* Meanwhile, my Life Skills class is graduating on Saturday. I have almost finished all the preparation. The certificates are signed, but there are a few more copies I have to make. My friends take over the packing while I find an officer to make the copies.

Finally, it's done and I hand it all over to my two best students with instructions on how to handle the graduation without me. By the time I get back to my cube, everything is packed, a mountain of blue bags and boxes. I have a ton of stuff. I have material for Life Skills, GED, and Cottage Industries (a program that allows inmates to earn extra income by doing arts and crafts) as well as the normal stuff an inmate collects over six and a half years. Surrounded by boxes, I do not sleep a wink, tossing and turning, worrying about what is in store. Usually in ADC, change does not bode well.

At 4:30 the next morning, I shower and begin the wait. At six I am sitting at breakfast when the officer yells at me to go to the V-gate for a trip to the hospital. I know the provider has ordered a bone density test, but surely not today. Yes, today. Staff assures me I'll be back and then move later and by the way, "You're going to San Pedro." My over-active mind shifts gears. Who in the world do I know there? My palms feel sweaty and my heart starts to race.

At the V-gate, I wait in the cold wind until the officer takes pity and allows me to go back to the warmth of the dorm. Finally, Transportation arrives. I am cuffed and shackled but, after so many of these trips, it is second nature. I am pleased to have company, a middle-aged woman from Santa Cruz just recently diagnosed with breast cancer who knows nothing about the disease and what to expect. She's started chemo and doesn't know about the chemo diet or getting a beanie to protect her soon-to-be-bald head. Thankfully, I am able to give her information about how to handle the journey she is now on, as well as give her names of people on Santa Cruz I know will help her. Helping her eases my anxiety about my move.

Our trip is routine and we are back at the prison in time for eleven o'clock count. However, I am not returned to Piestewa; I am taken straight to San Pedro and dumped at the V-gate. Eleven o'clock count has just started and I cannot go in. Shivering in the cold wind, I stand at the gate. Forty-five minutes later, the officer finally allows me to step into her guardhouse to warm my frozen body. I am chilled to the bone. If this move is for my health, this is not a great beginning. Count finally clears at noon and I am officially on San Pedro.

I begin a three-week field trip that becomes another lesson in gratitude. San Pedro was built thirty years ago to accommodate nearly 400 inmates. Due to overcrowding, the second kitchen now houses an extra fifty women with one toilet and two sinks. The classrooms on the sides of the buildings each hold ten more. They brought in Port-a-Jons for these extra women. A yard built for 400 now houses 500. The cafeteria has a capacity of sixty-four. Imagine feeding nearly 400 women per meal. The staff is constantly yelling, "Hurry up, hurry up, and move out." Gobble, gobble; ten minute meals. Welcome to Pedro.

I get my room assignment and begin the search for my stuff. It is at the sally port (the name for entry and exit gates bastardized from the French for *exit door*.) It is all piled up and waiting for inspection. But there is no inspection. I am told to just get it out of there. I am stunned but delighted; I hate those inspections. I have chronos for my extra stuff, but it's still a hassle to explain it all. This is a blessing. And there's another one. I run into a friend who has been on this yard a long time and has a very privileged job. She knows the ropes and gets things done. She takes over and commandeers some carts to ferry my stuff across the yard to my cell.

Thankfully, my new bunkie has just arrived from R & A. She has nothing of her own, so there is plenty of room for my stuff. I manage to cram it all in except for the bag with the Cottage Industries materials. I know Cottage Industries doesn't exist at Pedro so I head for the Programs Office to ask what I should do with it. The C.O.IV tells me I must see the Captain, but on the day before Thanksgiving she's gone. "Just hold on to it until Friday." Right before a holiday, no one is interested or they would have been more alert. I do needlepoint for Cottage Industries and needles are a red flag for would-be tattoo artists. On this yard, that stuff is contraband and I could be in big trouble if an officer in a bad mood decides to make my life difficult. Fortunately, no one does.

I make it back to the room for four o'clock count and then have time to study my surroundings. I know this room. I lived in one just like it for five years on Cruz. Only this one hasn't been painted for years and is dark and dingy. It is cold, and the rain this morning makes the concrete damp and clammy. I keep on my beanie and wrap a t-shirt around my neck. Thank God, I just did my laundry at Piestewa so all my clothes are clean. My bunkie tells me not to send my clothes to the laundry here. There is a big theft problem. I don't intend to be here long so maybe I won't need the laundry.

I spend the next few days getting adjusted to the chill, the very long lines, and the unemployment. I finally take care of the Cottage Industries stuff. There are three sergeants here from Cruz who know me and know I am not a troublemaker. They put my supplies in storage. They don't think I'll be here long either. One problem solved.

Next problem, no job. But another blessing crops up. One of the GED teachers used to be an officer at Santa Cruz. She's a lovely young woman I always respected. She hires me right away. Another problem solved.

The job is a blessing, but I want to get out of here. I spend my days slogging around in the mud, chilled, damp, and dirty. I wash my sweatshirt in the sink. The authorities have drilled holes in the wastebaskets, the washer of choice for all inmates. That is incredibly mean-spirited. It doesn't stop the washing; it just moves it to the sink. Of course, that means you never really get it clean or adequately rinsed. I hang it on the make-shift clothesline and it takes two and a half days to dry. I think longingly of pulling warm clothes out of a hot dryer at Piestewa.

I learn that my file suddenly has Medical restrictions on it. When I moved to Piestewa a year and a half ago, there were no restrictions, so where did these come from? The person in charge of all health issues at a prison is called the Facility Health Administrator (FHA). He is generally the invisible man, never seen on the yards. He is the answer to my problem. He can lift the restrictions.

I remember this FHA. Right after Gina died, ADC organized a Community Meeting to discuss all our grievances. There were many. Everyone was frustrated and angry and tempers flared. At the time, I spoke up, saying Gina would not have wanted us to yell at each other. We should be building bridges. We needed to be working together to make sure this doesn't happen again. How could we work together?

The current FHA was at that meeting. Suddenly, a miracle! He is standing in front of me on Pedro. Fearful yet determined, I approach him. To my astonishment, he remembers me and my part in that meeting so long ago. I tell him what has happened, not just to me, but to others as well who didn't deserve to be moved. He agrees to look into it. Later, I learned that he lifted the restrictions immediately. I am so grateful.

Now I just have to get back. I track down the head of programs to ask him to help. I ask my friends to send emails to the Deputy Warden. I feel then that it is just a matter of time but I am hoping to get back before Christmas. The holidays on Piestewa are actually festive because the DW there loves to decorate and make things pretty. On Pedro, the decorations are sparse and sad.

Meanwhile, I work. The supervising teacher works afternoons and evenings, leaving me free in the mornings to take care of all the business that crops up in prison. There is actually a lot because ADC loves paperwork and files. I enjoy the teaching; it's the cold, damp, long lines that wear me out.

Finally, a friend in the programs office sneaks word to me that she has seen my name on the pack up list. I should be going tomorrow. Thank God. Of course, I can't tell anyone that I know this top secret info, but I do begin to reorganize my stuff. On most yards, the officer brings the blue bag about six in the evening. Not here. On San Pedro they bring it very late. In my case, it is one in the morning when the knock comes.

It is pouring rain and the officer hands me a blue bag. I tell her that when I came I had five blue bags and she very nicely says she'll try to find some more. Thirty minutes later she is back with two more bags, soaking wet. My poor bunkie is now grumpy because she has to go to work in the kitchen in an hour. I decide I can pack after she leaves so I go back to bed and spend the time tossing and turning.

After she leaves, I hang up the wet bags and turn my fan on them. Now the icy room is icy and windy. I pack the one dry bag and start on the boxes. About five, the other bags are dry so I can pack them with my hygiene and food. I trek through the rain and mud to breakfast and finally, at seven I go up to the yard office to ask the sergeant for my Cottage Industries stuff they stored three weeks ago. I remind them how much stuff I have and ask how to get it to the v-gate. "Don't worry. Just get some inmates to help you." That is the answer to everything. *Cheap inmate labor.*

I ask the officers on duty to help line up some inmates and we are in the middle of this when the movement officer approaches us like a rampaging elephant. The other officers know her reputation and suddenly they fade into the background and are gone. She is furious that I have so much stuff. She yells at me like I am a recalcitrant five year old. Usually, I keep my head down and take whatever they dish out. This time I defend myself. I tell her that several days ago, I asked the Captain to facilitate this move because I knew it would be a problem. The Captain assured me they were well equipped to handle anything. I also told the sergeants. Same uninterested response. So I was doing the best I could and I was sorry. Like all bullies, she backs off. Somehow, with the help of inmate labor slogging through the mud and rain, it all gets up to the v-gate where we load the van and are finally on our way to Piestewa.

I am soaked and chilled, but so thankful to be away from there. At Piestewa, I leap out of the van. One of our stricter officers is at the gate and I want to hug her, but that is against every rule. I want to hug everyone. I am enthusiastically greeted by friends and former students glad to see me back. When I finally hit the bay, I immediately aim for the laundry room. I want clean, warm clothes. There is no line for lunch. There is no line for mail. It is dry and warm and wonderful.

This three-week field trip was indeed a lesson in gratitude. In our country, we always want more. The more we have, the more we complain about what we don't have. I spent five years on Santa Cruz and I remembered the oppressive heat, but I had forgotten the long lines, the damp cells in the winter, and the cold that permeates everything. It is miserable there. The trip taught me to count my blessings, each small but significant blessing. Taking warm clothes from a hot dryer is absolutely wonderful. Just being dry is divine. Being treated with kindness is like a warm blanket of comfort. When you open your mouth to complain about something, think instead of blessings, small, wonderful blessings. Life is full of blessings . . . *inside and out.*

Chapter 41

Apples, Suicide and Parole

March 2008. I am a people person. Even as a little girl, I would talk to anybody, anywhere, anytime. Mother said my favorite line as a three year old was "My name is Sue Ellen Allen and you can buy me a coke if you want to." That actually worked. However, there is a downside to being a people person. I care what people think. I care way too much what people think, always have.

You'd think at my age I'd be over it. I do think I'm better than I was, but the negative prison environment didn't help and parole board appearances sent me into days of anguish. After I'd served five years of my sentence, I had the opportunity to appear twice a year in front of complete strangers who didn't know me, but would be deciding my future. The first time I went I was naïve and optimistic. After all, I had a perfect prison record, I wasn't a trouble maker, and I'd started some very positive programs. Surely, I would be granted parole.

Well, not exactly. Every appearance was always about two hours of listening to people, especially the prosecutor, talk about what a horror of a human being I was. I was the Bonnie of Bonnie and Clyde for the financial world. I was a financial murderer. The second I was released, I would reoffend. Word by word, they slowly peeled the skin off my worthless body and then sent me back to the hell I deserved. A friend who had been through the same thing said she completely understood my despair.

"Listen, Sue Ellen, if everything the prosecution said was true, we would indeed be monsters and not deserve to live. But it's not true. It's just their job to paint us as completely black in a black and white world with absolutely no shades of grey."

Nevertheless, I took it to heart. Was this really me? At best: insensitive, selfish, superficial; at worst: hateful, greedy, mean-spirited? I couldn't bear to think of it. I relived every moment of my life, remembering all the thoughtless things I ever did. There were plenty, but there was also a little voice inside my head.

"That's not who you are. You know who you are. You know you've never in your life plotted to hurt anyone or be mean. "

There is no question I have hurt people. I used to have a very sharp tongue and would unleash it without any provocation. It was completely thoughtless and too often hurtful. I'm ashamed of that and now very aware that this kind of thoughtlessness and insensitivity is completely unacceptable. I never planned to be unkind. It's called thoughtlessness for a reason. I do believe I am more thoughtful now and more compassionate. I found that in prison and it feels good.

So what does all this have to do with apples? After the first parole hearing, I felt terribly depressed. Prison is a dark place anyway and their shockingly mean-spirited attack devastated me. I didn't expect them to retry the case. I thought they would look at what I'd done in prison over five years, and see what my positive plans were for the future. That did not happen. They focused on my admission of guilt. They wanted me to say I knew what David had been doing. I stressed that I accepted responsibility for the entire disaster because I should have known, but I did not know. However, I said if they wanted me to tell a lie, I would be there a long time. I was not going to live with their lie just for my freedom. To say they were not pleased is an understatement.

I thought of suicide. I was never going to get out of prison. I was probably going to die here. I was worthless and useless. Death seemed like a blessed relief. But how? Not a weapon in sight. Well, not true. There were possibilities, but I had seen what happened to others who tried it. Generally, they were just hauled off to CDU, the holding area for troublesome inmates. There was no comfort for despair and no counseling. Didn't want that.

I read that cyanide is the perfect medium for suicide and that apple seeds are full of cyanide. Normally, when we got fruit, we got old oranges, but there must have been a glut of apples because suddenly we were getting apples. I figured I could save the seeds and it would be a nice tidy end. No muss, no fuss.

Then my common sense set in and I started to wonder. How many seeds would I need to save? Ten? Twenty? Fifty? How many

apples would that be? How long would it take to save up a successful stash? Days? Weeks? Without internet access, I had no idea
and I couldn't exactly ask a friend to research it for me. I could see
it now.

*Dear Carolyn, I'm thinking of suicide. Could you please go to
Wikipedia and find out how many apple seeds I would need.*

The despair of the moment dissolved into dark humor. Not only
were things not as bleak, I began to think of the consequences of
my action. If I saved the apple seeds and successfully killed myself, they would never serve apples in the cafeteria again. Everyone
would suffer for my thoughtless, selfish deed. Those pesky words
again, thoughtless and selfish.

Suddenly I'd had enough of those words. I had no idea when
I'd get out, but I did have a life here. I was blessed to teach and
be useful. People depended on me. My husband would be devastated and would blame himself. My friends would be terribly hurt.
Besides that, I am alive. I survived the mastectomy under horrific
conditions AND chemo AND radiation. I AM ALIVE. How dare I
even think of ending my life regardless of the circumstances?

So I picked myself up and kept going to the board. Like the
rubber clown with the sand in his base who always pops back up
when you hit him, I kept popping back up. It wasn't easy and it
hurt a lot, but I kept popping and finally, on January 26, 2009, the
board granted my parole. I'd been sitting in the little chair in front
of them and when they told me I was going to be released, I sucked
in an enormous gasp of air. I realized then that I'd been holding my
breath.

I was supposed to sit very still, but I trembled as the tears
coursed down my face. The whole thing is a blur, but I will never
forget the joy of knowing I would soon be free. When it was over,
my friends who'd come to speak for me were hugging me and the
officers were turning a blind eye. We were giddy. I carried that giddiness back to the yard and shared it with everyone, inmates and
staff. My upcoming freedom is a symbol of hope for others and
everyone rejoices.

Now the waiting begins. The process of being released from the
custody of the state is no easy task and takes weeks or in my case,
months. One day, nearly two months later, I am summoned to the
deputy warden's office. It has been an unusually long time since

the board granted my release and I am beginning to believe it is all a cruel joke.

When the DW tells me to come in and close the door, my heart sinks. "Sit down," she says, and my heart sinks further. "You're going home tomorrow." Again, I gasp for breath and start to shake as the tears run down my face. Kindly, she shares my joy and allows me to call my friend who is planning to pick me up. No answer. I call two other friends. No answer. This is the moment everyone has been waiting for and there is no answer! It wasn't until later that evening that I finally reach Carolyn and arrangements are made. Reality begins to set in.

I do not sleep that night. There's been a lot of hugging and crying. Of course, inmates aren't allowed to hug, but staff was turning a blind eye except one grumpy officer. "Knock it off or I'll be writing tickets for the ones left behind." How sad to be in her skin.

There is a procedure to packing up. Everything is inventoried to make sure you are not giving anything away to your friends. My possessions are loaded on a cart and taken up front. I have my clothes for the next day and basic hygiene.

Lights go out in the dorm and I am left with my thoughts and my memories. Seven years of an unbelievable journey. Seven years of the slumber party from hell. Only it wasn't all hell. It was never heaven, but there are memories I would not trade, memories that will guide and define the next part of my life. On March 18, 2009, I stepped through the huge chain gate that separates inmates from the free world and felt like I had been shot out of a canon.

Gina's death started this memoir and Gina's death started the next part of my life. She gave me my passion and my purpose through the organization her parents started called GINA's Team. It's an acronym for Getting Inmates Needs Addressed and our vision is two fold. First, we want to bring community leaders, speakers, and educators into prisons all over the world to teach life skills courses and change lives so that their re-entry will be better. Second, we want to advocate for inmates like Gina who are ill and ignored. Her parents' fervent wish is for no more unnecessary deaths and suffering like Gina's.

Inside inmates are told that no one cares about them, that they are part of a forgotten world. It's practically a mantra: *nobody cares, nobody cares.* But I have found, on the contrary, that many people care. GINA's Team has a wealth of community leaders eager to donate their time at our prisons. We have a team of interns from Arizona State University who are dedicated to making a difference in the lives of the very many in this country behind the walls. Daily, they delight me with their energy, enthusiasm, and dedication to making a difference. They have adopted my motto:

Been there.
Done that.
Now how can I help?

That's my message to you. Everyone has a story. Everyone. No matter who you are and what your circumstances, you have a story and you have the power to use that story to help someone else. If you've been abused, you can help someone else who is beaten, afraid, and struggling. If you've lost a child, you can help someone else who is grieving. If you're an addict, you can help someone else come clean.

I believe we must take the pain, the grief, the fear, and the anger from our journeys and turn it into power. Turn the pain into power — power to help others who are lost or hopeless or terrified or angry, power to comfort and love. If you've been there and you've done that, you are the perfect person to help the next one in line.

So that's my story. Perhaps it will inspire you to begin a conversation with yourself on how you can use your story to help others. Or perhaps the conversation will be with your local officials on how we as a society choose to punish people. Elie Wiesel said:

"I swore never to be silent whenever and wherever human beings endure suffering and humiliation. We must always take sides. Neutrality helps the oppressor, never the victim. Silence encourages the tormentor, never the tormented."

People ask me what I want from writing this memoir. That is the perfect question. I want you to feel empowered and impassioned about your own voice and your own cause. You may not share my passion, but look deep into your soul to find what is hiding there, waiting to turn the pain into power, waiting to help the victim as well as the tormented. You have a voice for such conversation. I urge you to use it. The world is waiting . . . *inside and out.*

When I got out, I went on-line to get the real scoop on apples and cyanide. Here is the straight skinny:

"Apples are one fruit with naturally occurring poisons: their seeds contain amygdaline, a cyanide and sugar compound that degrades into hydrogen cyanide when metabolized. Cyanide itself is a poison that kills by denying blood the ability to carry oxygen and thereby causes its victims to die of asphyxiation. Once a fatal dose has been ingested, there is no effective antidote, and death takes place within minutes.

HOWEVER, *luckily for those fond of their Granny Smiths, the body can detoxify cyanide in small doses, and the number of apple seeds it takes to pack a lethal punch is therefore* ***huge***.

Apple pips also have a tough protective coating which makes swallowing them even less of a risky proposition; unless the pips are pulverized or masticated, the amygdaline they house remains safely contained within. Apple pips have hard, durable shells that allow them to pass intact through the digestive systems of animals, a quality which helps the apple to reproduce by distributing its seeds to new locations far from the originating trees. Were apple pips susceptible to the eroding effects of digestive juices, apple trees could not reproduce nearly as well as they do — their seeds would not be so widely spread, and a good many of the pips would be destroyed before germinating."

So enjoy your apples and forget about suicide. Even in prison, LIFE is worth living.

Conclusion
Life Begins Again

Life after prison is exactly like being shot out of a canon. Prison life is very, very slow. It is the ultimate in irony that the most precious commodity in the outside world is Time and yet that is what the State awards (odd use of the word) to punish inmates — Time. Why would you give the most precious thing there is to the people whom you most disdain? I'm just askin'.

On March 18th, I was shot out of that canon and I feel like the canon ball is still at its high arch. My entire time in prison, I conducted my own private conversation with God. More like a monologue, because it felt pretty one-sided. Usually I had my finger pointed in the air and was saying something like:

"God, if you want GINA's Team to work and you want us to bring programs back into the prisons and you want us to make a difference, then you better pave the way and open the doors. You better make it happen!"

It's a good thing God has a sense of humor and infinite patience with the likes of me.

I did have complete faith that God would indeed pave the way. I believed that the vision Diane and I shared was right and events since my release have proven that is true. One day a few months after my release Chris, Diane's husband, said,

"Sue Ellen, God isn't opening doors for you. God is knocking them down with a canon."

Within two months of my release, I was at a Memorial Service for Marcia Powell, an inmate who had died tragically at Perryville. The Director of ADC, Charles Ryan, was also there and, gathering all my courage, I approached him about GINA's Team. I introduced myself and told him I had some ideas for programming that wouldn't cost ADC anything. I knew he was faced with enormous budget cuts and this might be interesting. To my great surprise, he handed me his card and said to get in touch. Privately I thought he was just being polite, but I pocketed the card with every intention of using it.

The following day, Sunday morning before church, I e-mailed

him and within 45 minutes, there was a response with directions to call his assistant for an appointment. I was impressed and called the following day. The appointment was made.

In the meantime, I was at an ASU function for a group of educators where I found myself standing next to a well-dressed and very important looking man as we both balanced plates of breakfast food.

"Hi," I said. "I'm Sue Ellen Allen and I just got out of prison."

"Well, hi yourself. You certainly don't hear that every day."

It turned out to be another one of those introductions made by Divine Providence. Cecil Ash is a State Legislator and the vice-chairman of the Judiciary Committee. I told him of GINA's Team and our vision to bring programs into the prisons. I told him of our upcoming meeting with the Director and he said he'd like to come to that meeting. "OK," I said and we agreed to meet so I could brief him on our plan. Now, what are the odds of this unless someone with a much bigger picture is helping things along?

But wait, there's more. Our meeting with the director went very well and, thanks to the support of Representative Ash, two months later our proposal for a pilot program at Perryville was approved. Have you ever had a dream of something you wanted passionately to do and finally you get the green light? That's what happened and suddenly my heart fell to my knees. Now what do I do? Now I have to make it happen.

Shortly thereafter, Diane and I were sitting in the conference room of the Warden's office at Perryville Prison going over our plans with her staff. They were cordial and polite and I figured they were secretly wondering what we were going to do with this opportunity. It's time to make our vision happen. When Diane and I walked out of the prison that day, I said, "Gina lived in that room today. Gina would love this." And she would.

Fast forward a few months to January 2010. GINA's Team had its first successful event at Perryville, thanks to our very first volunteer, Misty Hyman. Misty is an Olympic Gold Medalist who won her gold in 2000 in Sydney for the 200 meter Butterfly. A lovely young woman, Misty was blown away by the reception she received from the women at Perryville

"I have spoken all over the country, to corporations and schools, and these women are without a doubt the best audience

I have ever had," she said.

Accompanying Misty was Raul Monreal, author, song-writer, and Director of South Mountain Community College who shared inspirational stories about his amazing life. The Warden and her team set the event up in an unprecedented way that was logistically quite difficult for them, but gave Misty and Raul three times the normal audience at Perryville. GINA's Team touched a lot of lives that night thanks to a unique collaboration. They are sharing our vision and we are grateful.

Then, to add balance to the Team, I was able to convince Representative Krysten Sinema and Representative Cecil Ash to go out to Perryville together and speak to the women about leadership and education, the first legislators to speak to a group of inmates. Both serve on the Judiciary Committee, representing the different parties. They provide us with opposing viewpoints and we provide them with a view of prison they would never see if they weren't on our team. We are all richer for it.

Early in the year, I met with Dr. Alesha Durfee, a professor at ASU who offered to publicize Gina's Team to her students. To my great surprise and delight, GINA's Team now has a group of interns from ASU whose enthusiasm and drive to make a difference in the prison world astonishes me. Recently, all these young women were in our living room, laughing and planning how to grow our Team from our grass-roots effort into a strong, focused organization.

Suddenly, my eyes welled up. Less than a year ago, I was an inmate in prison. Now I am hosting a group of brilliant and beautiful young women who are a part of Gina's Team. Our vision is coming true and through it, Gina lives.

Who would believe this could happen? I am a 64 year old woman who spent nearly seven years in prison. I lost everything material that people think matters. And yet, I am here to tell you to never, never give up on your dream. Believe it. See it. Work for it. With Divine Providence, anything is possible . . . *inside or out.*

When I Get Out

Before I was released, I made a list of all the things
I had dreamed of doing for seven years.

Listen to the sound of silence

Hear the birds

Pet a cat

Walk a dog

Sit on a soft sofa with pillows

Drink a glass of fresh juice

Eat all the fruits and veggies I want

Wear a skirt

Soak in colors other than orange and grey

Use real toilet paper without worrying it will run out

Wear perfume

Swim in a pool

Take a bubble bath

Shower in private

Use a telephone without restrictions

Listen to music without headphones

Go barefoot

Sleep on a real mattress

Have ice whenever I want

Drink from a real glass

Have a conversation that doesn't involve prison

Eat with a proper knife and fork

Go to church and sit in the silence

Go to a flower shop and just inhale the scent

Make a great big salad

Drink a proper cup of tea in a china cup

Dance all by myself

Sing in the shower

Wear earrings

Go to a movie

Eat using a proper napkin

Sit under a tree

Take long walks in lovely places

Surf the net

Go to the Art Museum

Go to the Library

Wear contact lenses

Dress up

Feel pretty

Drink real milk

Eat yogurt and fresh fruit

Dictionary of Prison Lingo

Submitted by Steven Downs

DW: Deputy Warden

ADW: Associate Deputy Warden

C.O.II: Uniformed corrections officers

C.O.III: A counselor who handles an inmate's records, programs, and issues

C.O.IV: Supervisor of the counselors, in charge of programs

MCSO: Maricopa County Sheriff's Office

MMC: Maricopa Medical Center

CPS: Child Protective Services

CDU: Central Detention Unit

A kite: A kite is prison slang for an inmate letter that is written to the authorities, used for many purposes. It is the only legal way an inmate has of communicating to staff. If you have a request or a problem, you write a kite so everything is documented. The reams of papers used are staggering.

Chrono: A permission slip that an inmate must carry for anything out of the ordinary. For example, if an inmate has a condition that requires a wheelchair, they must have a chrono. It is also written documentation of a change in your program status. It could be a job change, Medical appointment, etc.

The Hole: Disciplinary isolation that operates at super maximum custody level.

HNR: Health Needs Request. A Form for documenting Medical needs and concerns to the Medical department. If you need to see a provider about anything, including emergencies, you must submit an HNR..

Ticket: Disciplinary action that has a weighted impact on an inmate's progression through the system, depending on the severity. It's like a citation alleging a disciplinary violation. Results can mean job and privilege loss.

IMS: Incident Management System. It can be declared by a correctional officer or an employee. It begins when the person witnesses a potential interruption in the ordinary operation of the institution.

It has varying degrees of severity. First, there is a lockdown. Then there is a count. Next, it is determined if further action is necessary. Inmates fighting would constitute an IMS. Also an inmate having a seizure or passing out would cause one.

R & A: Reception & Assessment, the orientation period when you enter prison.

Old Number: The inmate has been inside a long time.

New number: Fish, newbie, any inmate who has just arrived or whose number is less than a year old. An old, old number is only 5 digits, like 054321. There are very few of them. My number is 172187. Now the numbers are in the 25000 range. There are about 40,000 inmates in ADC.

Brown: All staff.

Orange: All inmates.

Stinger: Metal coil sold at the store and used for heating water in a cup.

Slinging ink: The process of tattooing. Prison tattoos are strictly forbidden but happen anyway.

Home Boy or homey: A person from your neighborhood or the street.

The rack: Your bed.

Mattress sizing: One who lies around on their bed all day; a couch potato.

Hook up: A favor done for you by someone else.

No more: An inmate who has six days or less to the gate. (No more Sundays, no more Mondays, etc.)

Single Digit Midget: Inmate with nine or fewer days to the gate.

Pop or Mom: Senior member of the inmate population.

Shank: Homemade metal weapon used to stab someone.

O.G.: Original gangster. It's a term of endearment from a younger inmate to a senior inmate.

Baller: Inmate with a lot of money on his books.

Chow: Meal time.

Bones: Dominoes.

Watch-swallows: Medication that must be taken and swallowed in front of a nurse or officer.

Big Juice Card: Influence with staff.

Reading Group Guide

Sue Ellen Allen knew little of the system when she entered prison, but she learned. With our current system of incarceration, everyone suffers. The crime victim who believes the system doesn't serve them; the inmate whose sentence is draconian; the family who is broken by the punishment; the taxpayer who pays for excessive justice; the community who is divided by our views of crime and punishment.

Sue Ellen wants you to look at our system of incarceration and ask important questions about how it helps our society. After all, you are paying for it. You should know what is really going on.

1. What does she mean early on about being in a prison of your own making? Can you identify the type of prison in which you may find yourself? What would it take to break free of that prison?

2. Sue Ellen describes her experience as a difficult journey in a life full of journeys. She feels it enriched her life. Describe one of the journeys of your life that you didn't like but wouldn't trade.

3. Many times during her incarceration, she was faced with people telling her to give up yet she refused. Identify a time of great difficulty when you realized failure was not an option and you refused to quit. What happened?

4. When small things are taken away, we come to appreciate them. In several chapters, Sue Ellen writes about the small blessings for which she is grateful. What are some of the small things you take for granted that you would miss terribly if they were suddenly taken away?

5. In Chapter 2, Betrayal, Sue Ellen writes: *"My seven years there was a journey, the worst and most difficult in a life full of journeys. . . I learned who I am as a member of the human race. I learned that the only way forward is through forgiveness and love."* What do you know about forgiveness? How have you experienced it in your life? Did you do the forgiving or did you seek to be forgiven? What did you learn from the experience?

6. Many more people die in prison annually from inadequate healthcare than from the death penalty. You've read about the Medical treatment for Sue Ellen and Gina. Some people say inmates aren't entitled to health-care because many people on the outside can't afford it. Do you agree with that? How should we treat inmates, especially pregnant women and people with cancer? Should a minor crime end up as a death sentence?

7. In April 2001, Fortune magazine cited a study that explored three decades of prison college education; it found that every dollar spent on education resulted in $1.71 in reduced crime costs. " . . . *studies have shown that higher education behind bars dramatically reduces recidivism, which typically sits between 40 and 60 percent. According to a 1997 report by the Center on Crime, Communities and Culture at the Open Society Institute, inmates with at least two years of college education have a mere 10 percent rearrest rate."* Based on what you have read, how do you feel about education for inmates? Why should we give inmates an opportunity to learn?

8. From Calvin Beale, with the Economic Research Service of the U.S. Department of Agriculture: ". . . *throughout the 1960s and 70s, an average of just four new prisons had been built in rural areas each year. During the 1980s that figure increased to an annual average of 16 and in the 1990s, it jumped to 25 new prisons annually. Between 1990 and 1999, 245 prisons were built in rural and small town communties with a prison opening somewhere in rural America every fifteen days."*

From the National Resource Center on Prisons and Communities: "*By the end of 2001, one in every 37 adults in the U.S. had either done time in a prison or were incarcerated in a state or federal prison. If current incarceration rates hold, 6% of all Americans, 11% of all men, 17% of Hispanic men, and 32% of all African American men born in 2001 are likely to end up in prison at some point in their lifetime."*

From the Boston Globe: "*What is the 'world's leading prison state'? You might think it is China or Russia. But as a recent Pew Center study revealed, it is the United States where 2.3 million peo-*

ple — *one out of every 100 adults Americas — now languish behind bars. Per capita, our rate of imprisonment easily exceeds that of Russia, is six times that of China, and seven times that of Germany and France. Yet in an amazing act of hypocrisy, the State Department last week issued its annual Human Rights Report that condemned Russia, Burma, and China for arbitrarily imprisoning too many of its citizens. Nations that live in glass prisons should not throw stones."*

From The National Association of State Budget Officers:
" . . . *states spent a record $51.7 billion on corrections in FY2008, or 1 in every 15 general fund dollars. Adding local, federal and other funding brings the national correctional spending total to $68 billion.*

From The Pew Center on the States' Public Safety Performance Project: *"Violent and career criminals need to be locked up, and for a long time. But our research shows that prisons are housing too many people who can be managed safely and held accountable in the community at far lower cost,"* said Adam Gelb, director. *"New community supervision strategies and technologies need to be strengthened and expanded, not scaled back. Cutting them may appear to save a few dollars, but it doesn't. It will fuel the cycle of more crime, more victims, more arrests, more prosecutions, and still more imprisonment."*

The cost is staggering. It is now a multi-billion dollar industry that is doing very little to prepare inmates for release. Since 93% of all inmates will be released into the community, how do you feel about that? Would you prefer someone who has been locked up and forgotten or someone who has been prepared for a productive life?

Studies show there are many cost-effective alternatives to prison that would save money and do more for serious rehabilitation. Since we imprison more people per capita than Russia and China, why do you think this approach has not been popular with our American culture? We present ourselves as the most Christian, technologically advanced country in the world. Why do you think we support such an Old Testament approach of *an eye for an eye* to our system of punishment rather than the Christian one that Jesus espoused of complete forgiveness?

About GINA's Team

GINA's Team was founded by Gina's parents, Chris and Diane Panetta, in the fall of 2009. In the fall of 2010, it became a 501(C)(3).

Slogan: Getting Inmates Needs Addressed.

Mission statement:

GINA's Team gets inmates needs addressed by contributing to inmate education, programming, and re-entry, thus creating better citizens, smoother re-entry and more peaceful communities both inside and out.

Description:

GINA's Team, named for Gina Panetta who died while serving time in an Arizona prison, actively promotes education and self-sufficiency for the incarcerated in Arizona and the United States at no cost to the prisons. We bring volunteer community leaders, speakers, and educators into our prisons to teach Life Skills subjects. Our volunteer programs provide inmates with much needed tools for re-entry, provide community members as roll models, and allow volunteers to see inmates as human beings.

If you would like to know more about GINA's Team

www.ginasteam.org

ginasteam@hotmail.com

P.O. Box 36, Scottsdale, AZ 85252

Now How Can I Help?

As you can tell by now, my motto is very important to me, so important that I am formulating my next book about it. I will be telling stories of people who have had life changing "Been there. Done that." moments and turned their pain into power.

I would like to know:

* What was the life changing event?
* What did you learn?
* How did you find your passion within it?
* Did you resist it in any way?
* What helped you the most?
* Who are you helping now because of this event?
* How did that manifest?

Would you like to share your success with the world? Do you have a favorite quote that has inspired you? Sharing your pain can be difficult, but sharing the power you have created from it is compelling and persuasive. When you tell your story, you never know how many lives you will impact. Please share your stories with me and let's change some lives together. I would love to hear from you. Please write to me at:

Sue Ellen Allen
Now How Can I Help?
P.O. Box 36
Scottsdale, AZ 85252

theslumberpartyfromhell@gmail.com